CONSTRUCTING
WALLS, PATHS AND OUTBUILDINGS

Expert advice for all home owners on tackling a wide variety of building projects – from garden walls, storage bins and sheds, to drives and habitable extensions.

CONSTRUCTING WALLS, PATHS AND OUTBUILDINGS

Professional Advice for Tackling Small-scale Building
Projects

by
Alec C. Limon

693

THORSONS PUBLISHERS LIMITED
Wellingborough, Northamptonshire

First published 1979

ISBN 0 7225 0522 1 (paperback)
ISBN 0 7225 0523 X (hardback)

Photoset by Specialised Offset Services Limited, Liverpool
and printed in Great Britain by
Weatherby Woolnough, Wellingborough, Northamptonshire
on paper made from 100% re-cycled fibre
supplied by P.F. Bingham Ltd., Croydon, Surrey.

CONTENTS

1

GARDEN BRICKWORK

Bricklaying can be looked on as an arduous profession which takes a lot of muscle power to perform and a long time to learn, perhaps up to five or six years if it is to be done properly; but apart from being a trade or profession, laying bricks can have great therapeutic value. Bricklaying can provide the right amount of outdoor exercise for sedentary workers; in fact, men like Sir Winston Churchill and the late Denis Wheatley, author of many thrillers, found that relaxing with bricks provided all the exercise they needed.

Amateur Charm

Fortunately, garden brickwork takes its charm from its rustic appearance, so it is not necessary to be an expert. It is the moss and lichen which grow on the north side of the structure that make it attractive, not the even regularity of the brick courses. Neat, bright red brickwork looks garish in the garden and needs time to mellow, to settle and harmonize with the surroundings.

The amateur need not, therefore, be too distressed at his initial fumbling attempts which leave the courses uneven with mortar stains on the face of the bricks. Moss will soon grow on the roughness of the brickwork and cover marks that the professional bricklayer would call blemishes.

There are a number of small bricklaying jobs that can be carried out around the garden that will not only provide exercise but, at the same time, will help to provide a better environment in which to live and will help with our desire for at least a degree of self-sufficiency.

Serpentine Walls

As food prices rise with such monotonous regularity it becomes obvious that it is in our best interests to get the most out of our gardens. To do this we need sound paths that do not become waterlogged and unusable after a period of heavy rain, and we need sound walls that will form wind-breaks and make sun-traps to improve the production. These can be ornamental as well as functional. For instance, a serpentine wall makes an interesting feature and at the same time provides sun-traps on one side in which to grow outdoor tomatoes or other plants needing sun and warmth and against which fruit trees can be trained to grow.

On the opposite side of the wall more hardy plants which like shady places can be grown. This kind of wall is perhaps a little more difficult to set out than the ordinary straight wall, but it has the advantage that it needs no supporting piers, except at the ends, and not even there if the wall is only about 1m (3 ft) high. It is better if the walls are built to the maximum 2.1m (7 ft) height which is allowed without planning permission as fruit trees can then be trained to grow against them.

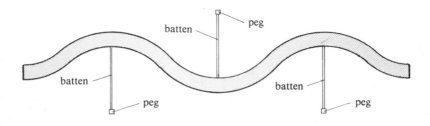

Plan of a serpentine wall showing the pegs and battens used to set out and maintain the arcs.

This kind of brickwork has to be done in a free-hand style as it is not possible to use a string line as a guide. A stout peg driven into the ground with a long batten tacked to the top of it, so that it can be swivelled around like the hand of a clock, will do to give a guide to the curves at the start. One peg and batten will be needed at each curved bay. The foundation will need to be as deep and the concrete as wide as for a straight wall of the same thickness. On sheltered sites a half brick 114mm ($4\frac{1}{2}$ in.) thickness will be enough for straight walls about 2m (6 ft) high, but on exposed sites where the wind resistance may be high it would be better to build walls one brick, 230mm (9 in.), thick. Also it would be wise to relieve the wind pressure by forming small openings in the wall in the hollow parts that face the prevailing wind. Small panels or short courses of decorative screen blocks would do the job and at the same time offer an attractive appearance.

Keeping in Shape
The wall will have to be kept in shape by plumbing it at regular intervals and a wooden template will be needed to lay on top of the

brickwork at each completed course so that the bricks can be adjusted to preserve the shape; but plumbing will still be necessary in order to keep the wall vertical.

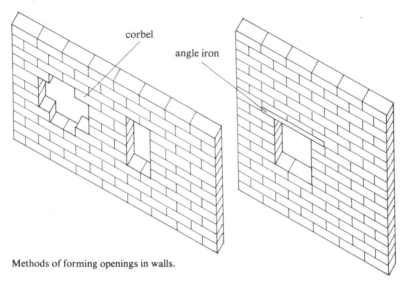

corbel

angle iron

Methods of forming openings in walls.

Another method of preserving the serpentine shape would be to use a pole instead of a stake and fasten the guide batten with a metal band around the pole so that it can be swivelled round and raised as the wall increases in height. This means that the pole needs to be firm and perfectly vertical in all directions otherwise the wall will soon be out of shape. Plumbing will still be necessary, as it is with all brickwork.

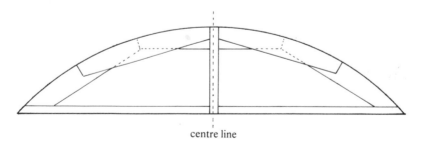

centre line

A template suitable for retaining the shape of the brickwork.

Boundary Walls

A serpentine wall is not suitable for boundaries, of course, because it means building partly on neighbouring land with one curve of the wall while the next curve cuts off some of your own land and gives it to your neighbour. This may not matter to two friendly neighbours, but serious legal problems may arise on the sale of either property.

High boundary walls may seem unsociable, but it is not necessary to enclose the whole garden. A high brick wall on the northern or eastern side of the site provides a sun trap and if the wall can be built on both the northern *and* eastern sides, so much the better. It will then provide a warm and sheltered place in which to grow and ripen fruit.

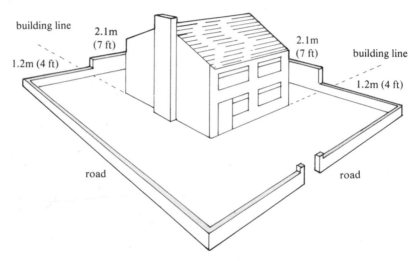

Permitted height of walls in front and behind the building line.

Walls can be built up to 2.1m (7 ft) at the rear of the house without planning permission, but these high walls must not encroach in front of the building line. The height limit for walls at the front of the house is 1.2m (4 ft).

These high walls need substantial foundations, and to stabilize them against wind resistance they need to have piers built at about 3m (10 ft) intervals. They will also need piers at each end. If the wall is to be 230mm (9 in.) thick, the piers can be up to 4m (13 ft) apart.

Because of its curves, a serpentine wall can be built 114mm (4½ in.)

thick as its shape is intrinsically strong and it can resist wind pressure better than the straight wall, especially if the curves are small in radius. A 2.1m (7 ft) straight wall, however, should be 230mm (9 in.) thick and it could have the same small openings, as for a serpentine wall, or short decorative screen block courses laid in the top third of the wall, to act as pressure relief valves.

The bricklaying process can be guided by string lines when building straight walls and it is therefore easier to get the bricks in line and keep the mortar joints even, but the bonding of the bricks at the piers has to be understood or there will be straight, vertical joints through the courses and they will weaken the structure. There are also bonding patterns which must be observed at the corners of the walls. These will be explained later.

Planting Beds
In urban areas where space is limited and often consists of only a concrete yard, a planting bed can be built in the sunniest corner. If the concrete base is not broken up, then weep holes will have to be provided at the vertical joints of the first course of bricks to let out the excess water which will accumulate during periods of bad weather. Without these holes the earth inside the bed will soon become saturated and the roots of the plants will rot.

The low walls of the bed can be built in 114mm (4½ in.) brickwork as they are rarely more than 300mm (1 ft) high. Low walls like these are ideal on sloping sites for preventing the soil being washed onto the paths. They can be used to divide the garden up into various areas and screen block walls can be built on top of them to form a decorative division between the vegetable garden and the flower garden.

Retaining Walls
Small retaining walls can be built to make a steeply-sloping site into terraces which will help to stop rain water washing the soil, and perhaps seeds, down to the bottom of the slope. High retaining walls, over about 600mm (2 ft), need careful designing and deep foundations if they are to withstand the pressure of the soil. All retaining walls should be at least 230mm (9 in.) thick. The insides of these walls and the insides of planter walls should be coated with a bituminous waterproofing material in order to help keep the bricks as dry as possible. Without the waterproofer the walls will always be wet from the soil on the inside and in winter the frost will cause the water to

freeze and expand and this will make the bricks and mortar crumble. Walls which are able to dry out between showers will withstand the winter weather better and last longer.

Another way of helping the walls to last longer is to lay coping stones on the top. These protecting slabs need not, of course, be stone; they can be cast in concrete. They should be wider than the wall so that they overhang each side by about 25mm to 38mm (1 to $1\frac{1}{2}$ in.). The underside of the overhang must have a groove or 'throat' cast in it as this will stop the water running back and trickling down the wall. In fact, this is the main purpose of the coping, the top of which can slope either to one side or to both sides; water will then run off the top and down the edge of the coping then under the edge until it reaches the groove: it will then drip clear of the wall, preventing the top of the wall from becoming saturated.

If copings are not available the top of the wall can be finished in bricks laid on their sides with their faces uppermost. This will turn the water better than the larger top or bottom 'bed' areas of the bricks, which are usually more porous than the face sides. If the wall is only 114mm ($4\frac{1}{2}$ in.) thick the coping bricks can be laid on end or they can be cut in half and the rough-cut ends bedded into the mortar. It stands to reason, of course, that smooth-faced bricks are better to use as copings than the rustic or rough-faced bricks, because they will not hold the water like the rougher bricks.

Trees
Although it is not the purpose of this book to give instructions on what plants or vegetables should be grown in the garden or even to suggest how to grow any vegetables, there are one or two points that should be made about trees.

Trees make effective wind-breaks and they are most decorative. Their presence gives the garden a rural air, but they have a far-reaching effect on the condition of the soil. A mature tree can take as much as 20,000 gallons of water from the soil in a year. This is no problem if there is a sufficient supply of water available without leaving other plants short of essential supplies and if the drying of the earth will not affect buildings.

The effect of so much drying-out of clay ground, however, can be disastrous, because clay shrinks considerably when it dries, as has been demonstrated during hot summers when the ground opens up in deep cracks. These cracks do not generally go deep enough to endanger house foundations, but when a tree starts to take such quantities of water out of the clay, then the drying process goes very deep and can weaken the load-bearing ability of the ground to such an extent that the foundations settle and cracks appear in the structure.

House foundations in clay ground are dug at least 1m (3 ft) deep to where the clay will be permanently wet and movement will be slight if there are no trees. Where there are nearby trees it will be necessary to take the foundations of any building much deeper. The same applies to high garden walls, if they are to be free from the ill effects of ground movement. It is therefore essential that trees are not planted nearer to a building than at least 9m (30 ft). Although their effect will not be apparent at first, it will be progressive and the drying of the area will become more serious as the tree grows.

The Water Table

The effect of trees on the water table, or ground-water level, works in reverse if an established tree is cut down. The enormous amount of water which the established tree has been taking from the ground collects when the tree has gone and this raises the water table. If the ground is clay, then it will swell as it takes up the excess water and this will raise the ground level itself. This clay heave is very powerful and can disrupt foundations or cause solid floors to lift and crack up.

Variations in water table in other types of soil are not so serious as they are more stable and damage may be confined to dampness of solid floors, if they have no damp-proof membrane.

It is obvious, therefore, that if there is an old-established tree on the site it should be left in place if it is possible for the building or other construction to be erected without cutting the tree down; the foundations must simply be made deeper. If the building is there first, then it is best not to plant trees near it.

There is still the problem of tree roots, which can be strong enough to damage foundations and disrupt drains. The way to tackle this is to prune the roots from time to time. This is not an easy task, but it is necessary.

Using Basic Bricklaying Skills

Once a little bricklaying skill has been obtained in building garden walls there are other uses to which it can be put. Dwarf walls for cold frames can be built in 114mm ($4\frac{1}{2}$ in.) brickwork on concrete strip foundations; similar walls and foundations are needed for greenhouses; brick sheds or outhouses are rather expensive, but are permanent and need less maintenance than wooden sheds – it is also possible to insulate the walls so that the room can be heated without running up excessive bills for heat wasted through the structure. Properly built brick walls that are rendered on the outside can be dry on the inside, at least sufficiently so for most storage purposes. For some uses it may be necessary to line the inside of the walls with a suitable material to improve the finish as well as the thermal insulation.

Paths
Walls are not the only things that can be constructed with bricks: they can also be used for making paths. In fact, the warm red colour of bricks lends a rustic touch that can never be achieved with concrete. This type of path needs a curb of some kind down each side to prevent the edge bricks from working loose, but the bricks themselves can be laid either in plain rows or to a pattern, depending on how much appearance matters, though with the domestic vegetable garden appearance is of as much value as utility.

Concrete has the advantage that it needs only temporary edge strips which can be removed as soon as the concrete has set. There are, of course, a number of textured finishes which can be given to the concrete to improve the otherwise stark grey appearance.

Crazy paving is another method of breaking up the stark look of the concrete. This can be marked on the surface of the nearly set concrete or crazy paving made of broken paving slabs, can be laid in mortar. Paving slabs of all sizes shapes and colours can be obtained, or you can make your own. These slabs can be laid on sand, or on a concrete base for heavy duty work such as drives.

Those people with gardens large enough to be called a smallholding will, of course, have a better opportunity to practise self-sufficiency than those who live in surburbia. Where there is sufficient space, it will be possible to keep small animals – if you know enough about keeping them, or are interested enough to learn.

Here again, building skills will be of service in providing pens and enclosures for the animals, as well as warm dry winter and sleeping quarters. Again, it is not the intention of this book to explain what animals to keep or how to look after them, only constructional information will be given.

2

REGULATIONS AND RESTRAINTS

Unless the deeds of the property contain special clauses which limit what may or may not be done, there are few regulations that have to be observed when building garden walls or laying paths. Extensions to the home and all other habitable buildings must comply strictly with the National Building Regulations (except for Scotland and central London which have their own regulations), which are designed to ensure that the structure is sound and that all reasonable fire precautions have been taken. Garages have to meet the fire regulations; sheds, stores and greenhouses come within the 'permitted buildings' category, but although there may not be any regulations governing the structure, plans of the proposed building must be presented to the local authority for their approval, as there are rules governing the siting of these buildings with regard to the boundaries, and the buildings may be rateable.

Height of Walls

The restriction of 2.1m (7 ft) on the height of walls at the rear of the building line has already been mentioned in the previous chapter and although an owner may be within his rights to build such a high wall all around his garden, it might well be considered anti-social. Of course, total enclosure is not essential. Sun-traps should be restricted to those parts of the garden where they will be most effective and the remainder of the wall can be kept to a lower level or small openings can be formed in large sun-traps so that neighbours are not entirely shut out.

The restriction imposed on the height of garden walls does not mean that there is an automatic requirement to fence the garden around. The land can remain quite open if the owner wishes. However, it would be foolish not to mark the boundaries with some kind of wall or fence, because without some formal line it would be difficult to prevent encroachment by others. Remember, too, that property used for a sufficiently long time without rent or restriction can be claimed.

Encroachment

Apart from height, the only other restriction placed on garden walls is that they should stand entirely on the owner's land and not encroach on neighbouring property. This means that the fence posts must be on the owner's land and this has given rise to the belief that a fence must face the neighbour's property and that it will be owned by the person whose land the fence posts face. This is not always true and it is quite permissible to build a fence with the best face (the palings) facing the owner's land. This has been done by some people and the only way to be sure who owns any particular fence is to look at the deeds of the property.

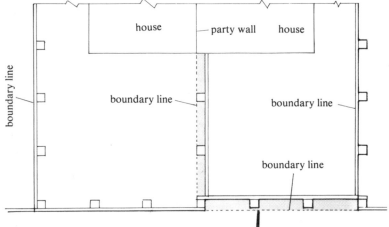

The effect of building a fence with the face side towards the owner's property, shaded parts virtually given to neighbour.

If it is decided to build a fence so that its face-side (or palings) faces the owner's land, then the small strip of land between the fence posts, or piers if it is a brick wall, will be excluded and may be used by the adjoining land owner. This may not seem important, but if for some reason the fence was to be changed to the conventional way round at some time after one house had been sold, then a dispute could arise over the exact position of the boundary.

Maintaining Boundaries

The exact position of boundary lines and ownership of fences can be hotly disputed and for this reason it is unwise to allow any situation to arise that may be misconstrued at a later date. For instance, it is permissible for the brick wall of a shed or garage to be built right up to the boundary line, but if that is done no part of the gutter or roof should be allowed to overhang the wall at that side, because it would project beyond the boundary over the neighbouring land.

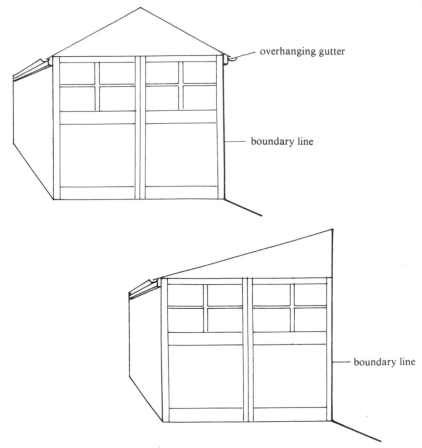

No part of a building should overhang the boundary.

Liberties like this should not be taken with other people's land and others should not be allowed to take similar liberties with your land just because they happen to be good friends of yours. At a later date problems can arise if a garage or shed is wanted on adjoining land which also has a right to be built on up to the boundary line. A friend may remove the gutter and make other arrangements for getting rid of the rainwater, but if the property has changed hands the new owner may take a lot of convincing that his garage gutter overhangs the boundary. He may insist that the line of gutter is the boundary line, which would in fact give a small strip of your garden to your new neighbour. It will save a lot of unpleasantness later if boundary lines are defined and adhered to.

Windows and the Right of Light

Legal tangles can be created when boundaries are ignored, even with the best of intentions, and this applies to windows too. They should not be placed in a wall that is built right up to the boundary line, not because of privacy or any restriction on the right to look across someone else's land, but because a window will acquire a right of light if it is allowed to remain long enough and this will then prevent anything else being built in front of it.

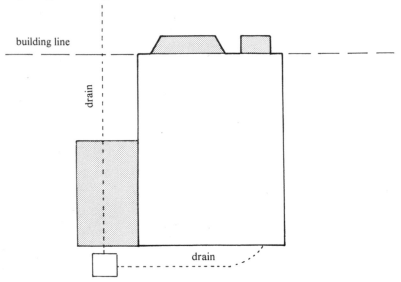

building line

drain

drain

A brick garage attached to a house must not cover a window. A drain beneath a building may have to be encased in concrete.

This right of light affects the building of high walls near to windows. Although no one has the right to a view, or to sunlight, or even to see the sky, they do have a right to sufficient light to carry out normal occupations in the room in question. For instance, a room is entitled to sufficient light for the occupiers to carry out all their domestic activities, even if there is no direct sunlight. If the room is generally used for meticulous work like sewing, then the owners will have the right to enough light to carry out that work without having to put on the electric light during the day; but it would have to be proved that this kind of work was being done regularly in the room without the use of artificial light before the wall or other obstruction was built.

The law can, of course, only be considered in general terms in order to avoid a possible clash. Each case is looked at in detail in court, but few people would want to go to the expense of testing their claims in court to find out exactly how far the law applies to their particular problem.

The interpretation of the Building Regulations is the prerogative of the local council and though these regulations are the same for all parts of the country, there is ample scope for considerable variation of that interpretation and its application. This accounts for the differences that occur in what may or may not be allowed from one council area to another.

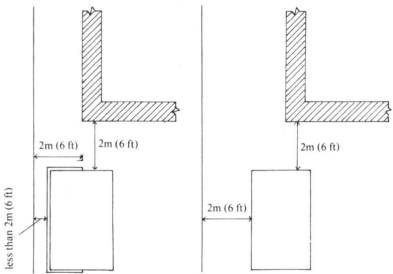

Those parts of a garage which are less than 2m (6 ft) from a boundary or building must be non-combustible.

There is no restriction on the walls of a garage built 2m (6 ft) or more from a house or boundary.

Garages

Garages do not have to comply with all the regulations as they come under the partially exempt category, but they do have to meet fire resistance requirements. A garage built of brick can be sited almost anywhere from the boundary to being attached to the house, but an attached garage must not cover a window and if there is a door into the house, then it must be half-hour fire-resistant and there must be a step, 100mm (4 in.) deep, down into the garage from the house. The roof of the garage must have a one hour resistance to fire and it appears that the regulations are concerned more with resisting fire from adjoining buildings and by flying fire brands than with resisting any fire that occurs within the garage.

This roofing regulation appears also to apply to all other types of building as well, but most of the common roofing materials like tiles, slates, asbestos and galvanized iron meet these requirements. The local Building Control Officer is able to give advice if it is proposed to use any unusual materials. Plans showing the elevation and a section through the structure together with a list of materials to be used should be submitted to the local authority for their approval.

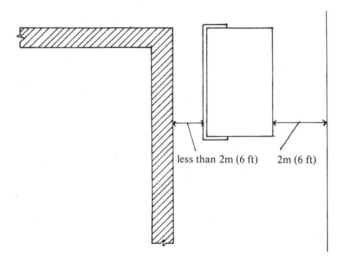

less than 2m (6 ft)   2m (6 ft)

The house side of this garage must be non-combustible; the boundary side need not.

These regulations apply to garages up to 40m² (430 sq. ft), which is big enough for two cars. Larger garages would not be considered as domestic. There is no restriction on the walls of the garage if it is built 2m (6 ft) or more away from the boundary and 2m (6 ft) away from any house within that boundary.

If the garage is to be closer than 2m (6 ft) to the boundary, then the wall or parts of walls that are within that limit must be built of brick or other non-combustible material. If there is a window in the house wall, the garage may not be sited within 2m (6 ft) of the house.

Habitable Extensions

Habitable extensions must comply with all the relevant building regulations. The main ones cover fire, ventilation, and insulation. The requirements for walls are similar to those already mentioned for garages, and this applies to roofs as well.

Ventilation must be provided equal to one twentieth of the floor area of the completed room. If there is a window at both ends of the room, then the opening lights in both windows can be included. Doors do not count when adding up the ventilation area. It is not essential to provide windows for the ventilation, although this is the most usual method: simple grills or other openings can be used.

Walls have to have a given standard of insulation and this requirement is most easily met by building brick cavity walls, but of course there are other constructions that are acceptable. These cavities can be filled with foam or other insulating materials to increase their effectiveness, provided, of course, that the filling does not allow water to pass from the outer to the inner leaf of the wall.

The requirements for insulating the roofs can be met by inserting 50mm (2 in.) of mineral wool between the ceiling joists, but of course a greater thickness will be more effective and will allow the central heating to be turned down and in that way save fuel and costs. There is a great deal of Government pressure at the moment to increase insulation in all parts of dwellings and so these requirements may well be increased again.

Another regulation which applies to habitable rooms is that of ceiling height, which must be not less than 2.3m (7ft 6in.). This rule does not seem to apply to kitchens, but dining kitchens would be included.

Fortunately, it is not necessary to know the whole of the Building Regulations in order to plan out what could be done with the house and garden. It is only when the detailed plans are made that this will be necessary. Most of the constructions required for increasing the productivity of the garden or for storage are outside the regulations and only need to be properly placed within the boundaries of the land. When it comes to designing a habitable extension, the work can be given to a professional if a study of the regulations seems to be a too formidable task.

Of course, if the entrance of the proposed extension is restricted to a simple doorway, instead of taking out the whole wall to make the extension part of the room itself, then it can be called a conservatory and will not have to meet all the regulations.

Glass-roofed conservatories are not suitable for use as extensions to kitchens as many people have found out who have tried to use them for this purpose. This is because the uninsulated roof suffers from very bad condensation whenever the weather is cold. It is this condensation problem that makes the conservatory only useful in the summer months, and in the winter no form of heating is ever effective.

3

FOUNDATIONS AND SETTING OUT

The principles involved in setting out buildings are quite simple and few pieces of equipment are necessary to carry out the work. Plenty of string is needed for marking the positions of the foundation trenches and the walls that are to be built in them. A steel tape should be used for making all the measurements in preference to the ordinary cloth tape, which tends to stretch.

A large wooden square is used to set the walls at right angles to each other and a long spirit level and a long wooden straight edge are also needed. Stout wooden stakes 50mm by 50mm (2 in. by 2 in.) are used to mark out the building and to support the 'profile boards'. These are boards fixed in line with the corners of the building on which the marks for the concrete foundation and the brickwork are made. A set of three tee-shaped 'boning rods' are also useful for levelling over long distances or setting out an even slope.

Clearing the Site
Before any building work can start, whether it is to be a simple garden wall or a home extension, all the vegetable matter must be removed from the site as well as all the top soil, or garden loam. Any large trees should be left in place, but if one has to be cut down, this should be done well in advance of building so that the ground water can rise and stabilize at its new level. Small trees that are too near the proposed structure should be removed before they become big enough to seriously affect the stability of the ground.

Using the 3:4:5 Formula
The large wooden square which is needed to set the corners of the building at right angles, can be made out of 25mm by 50mm (1 in. by 2 in.) batten using the 3:4:5 formula well known to all builders. Any triangle that has sides which bear the same length ratio as the numbers 3, 4 and 5 will have one right angle. Any unit of length can be used, i.e., centimetres, metres, feet or yards. A handy size of square would be 3ft by 4ft by 5ft (or using 300mm to the foot, 900mm by 1200mm by 1500mm). The three pieces of timber can be cut off to this length,

or the sides can be made a little longer if required as long as the third piece (the hypothenuse) is fixed in the correct place.

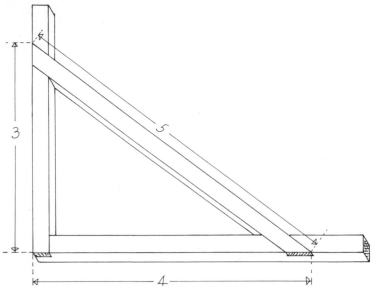

A builder's square made to the 3:4:5 formula.

A halved joint is made at one end of the two short battens and these are then screwed together temporarily with one screw. The longest length is then placed on top of the two side battens so that its outer corner is exactly in line with the outer corner of the two side pieces; or, if the sides have been cut longer than the ratio length, the batten corners must be in line with the 3 and 4 unit marks on the sides. All the pieces of timber can be marked so that halved joints can be cut, or the batten can be simply screwed on to the top of the side battens and the second screw can be driven into the first joint at the right angle.

For a strong job, the timber should be taken apart and the joints glued with a waterproof adhesive so that the square will not be affected by the weather and will withstand rough usage.

Setting Out

Setting out proceeds by fixing the profile boards in place. In the case of a garden wall these boards are set up at each end well clear of the brickwork so that they will not get in the way when building starts. The boards may be any length, but should be long enough to span the width of the foundation trench with enough to spare at each side to allow the supporting pegs to be out of the way. Keeping the profiles well clear of the trench is not so important if the digging is to be done by hand, but if a mechanical digger is to be brought into use (and this could be necessary if a long garden wall is to be built on clay ground where the foundations would have to be deep and the digging would be very hard work), the driver will need to have room to manoeuvre his machine without knocking the profiles down.

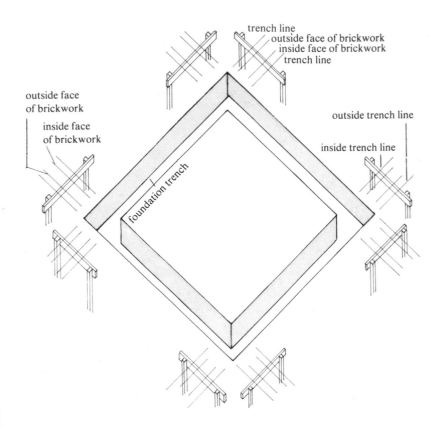

Foundation trenches, showing profile boards, trench lines and brickwork lines.

When setting out, the position of the front wall is determined first by measuring from the wall of the house. Care must be taken to ensure that the new wall is parallel to the existing wall. Temporary pegs can be driven into the ground to help in getting the profiles in the right place so that they will be well clear of the corners of the new building. The position of the sides of the extension are marked by nailing profile boards to the house wall a little above the damp-proof course level and in line with the proposed foundations.

On these profiles are marked the positions of the two leaves of the cavity wall and the width of the foundation trench. From these marks a line is squared across to give the position of the profiles for the other end of the side walls. These can then be set in place and the necessary marks made on them. The squareness of the setting out can then be checked by measuring the diagonals, which should, of course, be the same length. If necessary, adjustments must be made because any discrepancy at this stage could cause problems later. For instance, if the floor is to be covered with tiles they will show up the slightest irregularities in the straightness of the walls and in the squareness of the building.

When all the pencil lines have been made and checked for accuracy, they should be cut into the profile boards with a fine-toothed saw, so that they will be positive and will not get rubbed off.

Garden walls have to be positioned carefully to avoid encroaching on the neighbouring land. The walls can be lined up by measuring from the house walls to ensure that the garden wall is parallel to it. Where gardens are rectangular, measurements can be made from the opposite walls to get the new wall in its exact place, but it may be necessary to get a professional surveyor to use his theodolite to position irregular boundaries if the original markings have been allowed to decay or disappear.

Before digging the foundation trench for an extension or outbuilding, check that the structure will be square by measuring the diagonals. A string line can then be fixed to the outer mark on the profile boards to provide the necessary guide for digging the trench. If a mechanical digger is to be used, it will not be possible to provide a string as a guide and the line of the trench will have to be marked on the ground with lime, like marking a football pitch.

If the new building is to have a curve or a multi-sided projection in brickwork, then it would be best to make a wooden template, like the one suggested for use when building a serpentine wall, with a centre line marked on it. An axial line should then be pegged out with the rest of the foundations. The centre line of the template can then be set along the axial line so that the foundations can be marked and dug. The template should be the exact shape of the required brickwork as it will be needed to ensure the correct positioning of each course of bricks.

The alternative of a peg driven into the ground at the centre point of the curve, with a batten attached, as suggested for the serpentine wall, could be used. Of course, when the brickwork reaches the peg height this method of guiding the brickwork becomes ineffective, so a template will still be necessary for the higher courses.

Depth of Foundations

As far as garden walls are concerned, the foundations can be dug to any depth, but it is wise to take them to the same depth as the house foundations if the wall is to be built on clay ground. Whatever the state of the ground, the foundations must be below the garden soil level. When a habitable building, or an extension to a habitable building is to be built, the depth of the foundations may be marked on the plans, but they are finally agreed by the Building Control Officer who will visit the site to inspect the trench before any concrete is poured.

Both heights and depths are measured from some fixed point. When building extensions to property it is usual to use the damp-proof course as the 'datum' point. Where this is not convenient, a peg has to be driven into the ground and the top of this peg is then levelled with the damp-proof course. The peg should then be concreted into place so that it cannot be accidentally moved once it has been correctly levelled.

Setting Out for Large Buildings

Setting out for large buildings and levelling over long distances is best carried out by optical instruments like dumpy levels, but the average handyman can do the job quite efficiently using a builder's long level and a long straight edge. A set of three boning rods are useful too, as they can be used either to project a level line over a long distance or they can be used to project a long, straight gradient such as a path or drive.

Boning rods are simply two pieces of batten which are fixed together to form a tee-shape. They may be 3m (3 ft) or 1.2m (4 ft) high with the top 457mm (18 in.) to 600mm (24 in.) long.

These rods are used for levelling purposes by driving a second peg as far from the datum peg as the straight edge will allow and levelling the tops of the pegs. Then, with the aid of assistants, one boning rod is placed on the datum peg and another is placed on the second peg. A third peg can then be driven as far from these two fixed positions as required and the top of it is levelled by putting the third boning rod on the top of it and sighting over the top of the first two rods. When all the peg tops are level, all the tops of the boning rods will be in line.

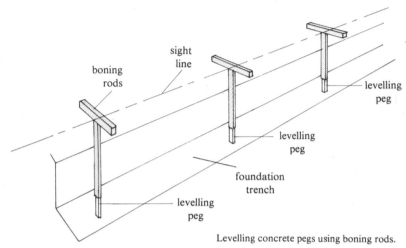

sight line

boning rods

levelling peg

levelling peg

foundation trench

levelling peg

Levelling concrete pegs using boning rods.

If the rods are less than 1m (3 ft) high, they will be awkward to use as they will cause a lot of stooping to sight over them. If they are more than 1.2m (4 ft) high they will be too long for ease of handling and sighting. The rods can be made out of 25mm by 75mm (1 in. by 3 in.) timber and the tops can be either half-lap jointed or morticed and tenoned. The latter method is necessary if there is a lot of levelling to carry out as it will stand up to rough usage better.

Digging the Foundation Trench

When digging the foundation trench it is important to ensure that the sides of the trench are straight and vertical, and that the bottom of the trench is clean and level. Levelling and measurement of the depth of the trench are done by driving wooden stakes into the bottom of the trench.

It is usual to make the top of the peg in the trench represent the top of the concrete for the foundation. So if the concrete is to be 1067mm (3 ft 6 in.) below the damp-proof course level, which is the usual datum, then a straight-edged board is packed up level across the trench from the datum peg. Beneath it another peg is driven into the bottom of the trench until the top of this peg is 1067mm (3 ft 6 in.) below the bottom edge of the straight edge. If the concrete for the foundation is to be 150mm (6 in.) thick, then the bottom of the trench has to be carefully dug out until it is 150mm (6 in.) below the top of the peg.

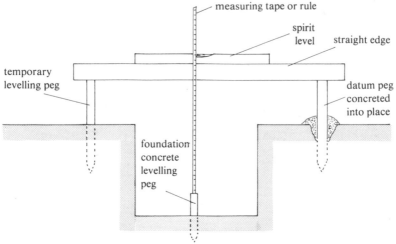

Measuring the depth of foundations to the top of the concrete from the datum peg.

Another peg is then driven into the bottom of the trench as far from the first one as the length of the straight edge, which is then used with a long level to bring the new peg top to the same level as the first one. This is carried out from one end of the trench to the other. In the case of an extension or rectangular building, pegs are driven at each corner and along the length of the trench if necessary.

When the level pegs have been positioned, the bottom of the trench has been cleaned of loose material, and the sides are straight and smooth, the concrete can be poured in. No hardcore is ever put into foundations for walls. The concrete is placed directly onto the earth.

Mixing the Concrete
The mix to use is one part cement, two and a half parts sand, and four parts coarse aggregate. Cement can be bought in 50kg (1 cwt) bags and the sand which is bought loose should be 'sharp' (not the 'soft' or

builders' sand used for mortar). The most important point about it, and of all the materials, is that it should be clean and free from dirt and clay. The coarse aggregate can be either gravel or crushed stone, which varies in size from 4.5mm ($\frac{3}{16}$ in.) to 19mm ($\frac{3}{4}$ in.). In some parts of the country, especially where crushed stone is available, it is possible to get 'all-in' ballast. This is a combined aggregate and can be used for garden wall foundations and anywhere where the uniformity of the concrete is not of any real importance. But, generally, the use of separate aggregates which can be measured in exact proportions is better.

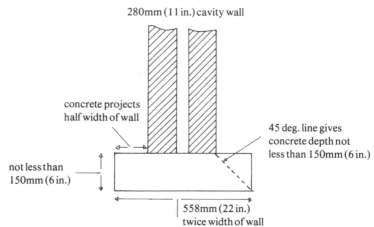

Calculating the depth of concrete slab.

Do not add too much water when mixing the concrete as this will weaken the finished product. Just use enough to wet all the ingredients and make the mix workable enough to place in the trench and compact down without leaving large air holes at the sides of the trench.

The actual size of the concrete slab required for the foundations depends on the width of the wall being built. It should be twice the width of the brickwork and the thickness is determined by making a scale drawing of a section through the wall and then drawing a line at 45 degrees from the face of the brickwork down through the concrete. Where this line meets the front edge of the concrete denotes the depth required. However, the depth of concrete should never be less than 150mm (6 in.). Also, the depth of the concrete should be at least equal to the amount of projection from the face of the brickwork.

Laying the Concrete

Concrete should not just be thrown into the trench and left. It should be laid carefully in layers about 100mm (4 in.) thick and each layer should be tamped or prodded with a stick to compact it and ensure that there are no holes in it. Continue placing the concrete until it reaches to the top of the pegs. It can be tamped with a straight edge until level with the top of the pegs. The pegs can then be pulled out and the holes they leave made good. This means that the pegs should not be driven too far into the bottom of the foundation trench or else their removal at this stage will not be very easy.

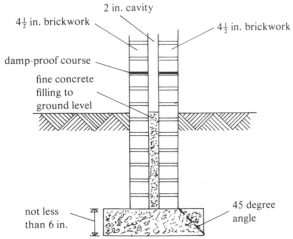

Foundations for an 11 inch cavity wall.

Laying bricks in the bottom of a narrow trench is not easy for a beginner and it is not necessary to restrict the concrete to only a few inches thick. It is possible to fill the trench with concrete right up to about ground level. The surface of the concrete must still be levelled off properly otherwise it will be very difficult to get the courses of bricks level. Even the cavity walls for a habitable extension have to be solid up to ground level, 150mm (6 in.) below the damp-proof course, so the concrete can be brought up to that height if required.

It is a good idea to check the local price of ready-mixed concrete as well as the cost of bricks, because it could be cheaper to use concrete, as many builders do, though their savings are mostly in labour charges. The handyman does not have this cost to find so his savings can only be on the cost of materials. The 230mm (9 in.) wide foundation concrete needed for a half brick 114mm ($4\frac{1}{2}$ in.) garden wall could be as cheap and probably very much easier to construct up to ground level in solid concrete, rather than struggle to lay bricks at the bottom of a deep and narrow trench.

Although it is unlikely that the amateur bricklayer would have to dig deeper than 1m (3 ft) a word of warning should be given. Any trench deeper than 1m to 1.2m (3 ft to 3 ft 6 in.) needs to have its sides supported with timber to prevent any accidental collapse onto the person working within it. Sand, gravels and other soft ground will need support at a less depth, but if the trench is not too deep then the lone worker will not be trapped by a sudden collapse of the sides and unable to get out unaided.

Angled Structures

Sometimes, walls have to be built at an angle, either for functional reasons or for decorative purposes. When this is necessary the setting out is done by means of a centre line in order to get the angles equal. If the walls form the lower part of a bay window, for instance, a wooden template can be made as a guide for laying the bricks, but a centre line will be needed to ensure that the template will be correctly positioned each time it is used.

Accurate setting out of buildings is important, and though any errors which are made at the foundation stage may not be very noticeable at first, when the floor tiles or ceiling tiles are being laid the squareness, or lack of it, of the building will show up considerably. It is quite impossible to lay square tiles in an out of square room without showing up the defects of the structure.

There are, however, times when it is necessary to put up structures that have angled walls and may not even have any right angles from

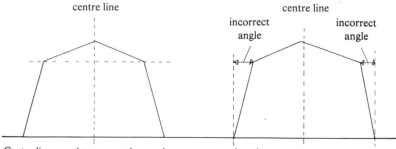

Centre lines used to ensure that angles are correct when there are no parallel walls.

which to check the setting out of the building. In this case the setting up of a centre-line is of great importance, in order to get the correct angles. Setting out lines need not necessarily be in the centre of the building. In some instances, when a new structure has to be built at a little distance from, and at an angle to, the house or main building, it will be necessary to project a string line from the main wall and in line with the main building so that measurements can be taken from it. This is very necessary when a new building such as a garage is to be built right up to the building line. The line is fixed at least 3m to 4m (10 ft to 13 ft) down the side of the existing wall and is then pulled tight for the length required. It is made to just touch the existing brickwork down its length and then it can be used as a setting out point.

4

MATERIALS AND BRICKLAYING

Before starting to do any bricklaying it is necessary to know a little about the materials which are used for building brick walls. First, the bricks.

Bricks

There are many types of clay for making bricks, but although the finished product from each type of clay will be different in colour and texture, good bricks of any type will have the same characteristics. They will all, for instance, be of the same size and they will be regular in shape, unless they are hand-made rustics whose charm lies not only in their colour and texture, but also in their irregularity. The edges should be sharp and when two bricks are knocked together they should ring with a slightly metalic sound. When a good quality brick is broken in two the inner surfaces should be uniform in appearance and have a granular texture.

Weathering Ability

Although colour and texture are important features when choosing bricks for a particular purpose, there is one more point which has to be considered: the weathering ability. New bricks will only be essential for construction work at the front of the house where appearance is of paramount importance. For most of the building work around the garden, such as wind-breaks, sun-traps and paths, second-hand bricks will be quite suitable. Bright new bricks would seem garish and out of place; old bricks soon weather so that they blend in with the garden scene.

Classes of Bricks

Buying second-hand bricks may mean that the choice is limited, but it will be necessary to know a little about the various kinds of bricks so that some degree of identification is possible. There are three main classes of bricks: commons, which are generally used for interior walls because they are soft and do not stand up to the weather well; facing bricks, which come in many types of finish from smooth-faced to rough rustics, including, of course, the expensive hand-made patterns; and, finally, there are the hard engineering bricks. This last type is not really suitable for use by the amateur and the beginner at bricklaying would find them very difficult to lay. This is because these bricks are very hard and difficult to cut. Also, because they are impervious, they do not take up water from the mortar with the result that they move about in the soft mortar after they have been laid, which makes them awkward to keep in a straight line and to maintain in a level course. If building with these bricks is attempted the mortar must be drier than is normally used for bricklaying.

The blue engineering bricks are easily identifiable – they are the type so widely used for walls and bridges on the railways. Red engineering bricks are not quite so obvious, but they can soon be identified by their weight and hardness. They weigh around 8 to 10 lb ($3\frac{1}{2}$ to $4\frac{1}{2}$ kg) and should not be confused with red facings which only weigh about 6 to 7 lb ($2\frac{3}{4}$ to $3\frac{1}{4}$ kg).

Perhaps the most prevalent of bricks is the fletton, which though it may be classified as a common, is frequently used for exterior walls where appearance is not of importance. Though machine textured facings such as wire-cut are used for the front walls of domestic property.

'Frogs'

Apart from textured facings, there are also bricks with dovetail-like slots in the faces. These are intended for plastering or rendering with cement and sand. The slot being to give the plaster more grip on the walls. Another pattern is the brick with a deep indent or 'frog' in one side. This makes the brick a little lighter and gives the mortar more grip. The correct way to lay these bricks is with the 'frog' upward so that it fills with the mortar. However, some builders lay these bricks with the frog down in order to save mortar. As far as domestic work goes it makes little difference to the strength of the wall which way up the brick is laid.

Some bricks which come from old buildings may have a number of holes through them. These serve the same purpose as the frog – they lighten the brick and offer a little extra grip for the mortar. This may be necessary when using the old-type lime and sand mortar, but the cement and sand mortars adhere very well and can be very difficult to get off the second-hand bricks.

Another type of brick which, though it may not be found in great quantities amongst second-hand bricks, has nevertheless been fashionable for some years, is the sand-lime. Unlike other bricks which are made of burned clay the sand-lime, as its name suggests, is made out of a mixture of sand and lime which is not burned, but moulded under pressure and then subjected to steam-pressure for many hours. If a colouring agent is not added the bricks are plain white.

The nominal size of a brick is 9 in. by $4\frac{1}{2}$ in. by 3 in., but in order to allow for the mortar joints the actual size of a brick is $8\frac{3}{4}$ in. by $4\frac{1}{4}$ in. by $2\frac{3}{4}$ in. There is also the metric brick which is 225mm by 112.5mm by 75mm nominal. Its actual size is 215mm by 102.5mm by 65mm, but it is not yet likely to be found amongst the second-hand bricks from demolition sites.

Cleaning Bricks

It may be possible to get the bricks cheaper if you offer to clean them yourself. Cement and sand mortar will be difficult to remove and a brick hammer will be needed. This has a square face and a long curved blade with a chisel end, or it can have detachable 'combs' which are serrated blades which fit into the end. This chisel end can be used for cutting bricks and for cleaning old mortar off them. Some of the oldest bricks may have been laid in lime and sand mortar and this can often be chopped off with the edge of a trowel fairly easily.

Making Mortar

Having obtained the bricks for the job, the next operation is to make the mortar for laying them. The most common type of mortar is made from cement and sand, the proportions of which vary depending on the type of brick being used. This is because the mortar should never be harder than the bricks. Use builders' or soft sand and, if the appearance of the finished work is of importance, ensure that it is an even light colour because it will affect the colour of the mortar. Either lime or a proprietary mortar plasticizer can be added to the mortar mix to make it easier to use, or 'more fatty' as a builder would say.

A good general mortar mix that will be suitable for internal or external walls is 1 part cement: 1 part lime: 5 parts sand. If a plasticizer is to be used, simply leave out the lime and add the plasticizer strictly in accordance with the maker's instructions.

The top of a free-standing wall should be protected with an overhanging coping, but it can be finished off with a course of bricks laid in slightly harder mortar to resist frost action in winter weather.

For this a mix of 1 part cement: $\frac{1}{2}$ part lime: 4 parts sand can be used. This stronger mix can also be used below ground level, especially where the ground is generally waterlogged. Even stronger mortar can be used with engineering bricks. With such hard bricks it can be strengthened to 1 part cement: $\frac{1}{4}$ part lime: 3 parts sand.

The amount of water used is largely a matter of common sense. The finished mortar should be soft enough to spread easily, but firm enough to be fashioned into a banana shape and picked up with the trowel. It should not squeeze out and run down the wall when bricks are bedded into it. When using a plasticizer, less water will be needed as the air in the mix reduces the amount necessary, so stop adding water as soon as the mortar becomes sufficiently workable.

For general garden work there is no need to make any fancy finishes, but when building extensions and other buildings there are cement colours which can be added to the mortar mixes for improved effects. Always use them in accordance with the instructions and gauge the ingredients accurately. When the mortar is wet it will be a little different, probably darker in colour, so it will not be possible to match each batch by its appearance. The colours can be obtained either as liquid or powder.

Do not mix more of any mortar than can be used in about an hour. After this time mortar which has started to set should not be remixed. This time limit varies according to the weather. On hot days when the sun dries the mortar quickly, an hour may be the limit, but on damp or humid days the mortar may stay workable for much longer.

Finishing off Joints
The mortar joints of the brickwork can be finished off in various ways according to the type of building. For a rustic appearance the mortar can be scraped off level with the face of the bricks and left to collect moss and algae. Most structural brickwork is given a 'struck' or 'weathered' finish by professional bricklayers. This means that the mortar is pressed in at the top of the joint, by the trowel, so that it slopes slightly to the face of the wall. By this method a small drip is formed under the top brick and rain is brought forward by the slope so that it runs down the face of the brick to the next drip, instead of soaking into the mortar.

There are various fancy ways of finishing off the joints, one of these being to run a piece of pipe along the mortar to form a curved recess and another is to rake out the mortar to a depth of not more than

12mm ($\frac{1}{2}$ in.). This latter method increases the shadow effect, which some people like, but as it encourages water to stand on the top of the bricks, where in winter it can freeze and cause damage, it is not suitable for walls in very exposed positions.

For very special work the joints can be raked out as suggested and then filled in, or pointed, with coloured mortar. Pointing should be carried out as the wall is being built, so that the pointing and the bed mortar become integral. Wait until the mortar has had time to set a little (new mortar will be too soft to hold a good shape), then fill in any hollows that have been left and at the same time cut off any mortar that may project beyond the face of the bricks. Point the vertical joints or perpends first, then the bed joints. Press the mortar into the required shape and then 'iron' it smooth with the trowel or a piece of pipe.

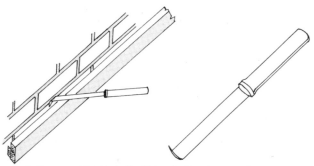

A frenchman made from an old table knife. Using the frenchman and a straight edge to trim off mortar.

The roughness of the mortar at the face of the brick is cut off with a tool called a 'frenchman'. It can be made from an old knife with the end filed to a triangular point and then turned at right angles to the blade. This tool is used with a small straight edge which has a piece of packing fixed at each end to hold it clear of the wall. This is so that the waste mortar can fall clear as it is cut away.

Laying Bricks
Laying bricks in neat courses takes a little practice, but it does not take long to master the principles. The corners of buildings or the ends

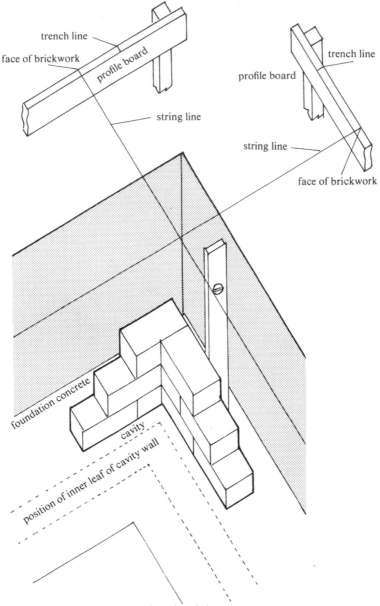

trench line

face of brickwork

profile board

string line

profile board

trench line

string line

face of brickwork

foundation concrete

cavity

position of inner leaf of cavity wall

Corner brickwork being built up from foundation concrete
plumbing down from string lines attached to the profiles.

of free standing walls are built first. They are raised about 600mm (2 ft), which is about eight courses, and then a string line is used as a guide for filling in between them. A length of batten marked with the brick and mortar joint thicknesses is used to ensure that each corner is raised to the same height as the others.

First, a string line is drawn tightly between the setting out profiles to mark the position of the wall. Then a bed of mortar is laid on the foundation concrete under the line. A brick can then be placed on the mortar and a builder's long level used to plumb down from the line to get the brick into its finished position. When the brick is directly under the line it can be levelled before the next brick is laid adjacent to it. Assuming that it is a 112mm ($4\frac{1}{2}$ in.) or half brick wall, about three or four bricks are laid end to end and carefully plumbed down from the line above. These bricks have a small amount of mortar placed on one end before being laid. This is to form the perpendicular joint.

If a corner is being raised, then three or four bricks are laid along the foundation at right angles and plumbed down in the same way. Then a second course is laid on top of them. This will provide the correct bond as the first brick of the second course will overlap, at right angles, the brick of the course below. If it is the end of a free-standing wall then a half brick will have to be laid in order to provide the correct bond or overlap of the bricks.

Bricklaying continues in this manner until the corner, or wall end, reaches about 600mm (2 ft). A great deal of care must be taken at this stage if the finished wall or building is to be soundly constructed and look presentable. Apart from levelling each brick as it is laid, a short straight edge or a builder's long level should be used to ensure that the whole of the course is level. This applies to the plumbing of the work as well. Do not just rely on plumbing each brick into line with the string above, but use a straight edge to ensure that the wall is not just in line with the string, but is also straight from top to bottom and does not show any hollows or bulges, either vertically or horizontally.

It is also necessary to try the gauge batten with its brick markings against the wall at the start of each course to ensure that the course and the mortar joints are uniform. When one corner or end has been raised to a sufficient height, work can start at the second corner. Here the gauge batten will ensure that each course is the same height above the foundation concrete as the courses of the first corner.

When two corners or ends have been raised, a string line can be stretched between them to mark the position of the top edge of the first course of bricks as a guide for filling in between the corners. Lay a bed of mortar on the concrete – this time there can be sufficient mortar for two or three bricks. Each one is buttered on the end with a small dab of mortar before being laid in place. Each brick is laid in the bed mortar and gently tapped down level with the string line.

All the brickwork should be built up until the level of the damp-proof course is reached. This is not less than 150mm (6 in.) above the ground level. At this point the brickwork should be checked to make sure that it is level right around the building. Continue to work round the building raising the corners and filling in the walls until the height for the door and window frames is reached. These are then propped into place where they are held plumb with battens until the brickwork is built up around them.

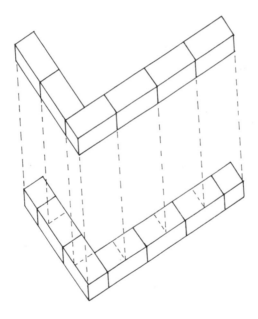

Simple stretcher bond. Half brick provides the bond. Dotted lines show position of next course.

Metal angle brackets are screwed to the frame sides so that they can be built into the mortar joints of the brickwork to hold the frames firmly in position.

Types of Bonds

For most garden walls half brick thickness is enough if piers are built at about 3m (10 ft) centres. This is simple *stretcher bond* and is maintained by putting a half brick at the beginning of every second course. The half brick can be provided by the corner brick, as already mentioned.

For greater strength a 225mm (9 in.) wall is needed and this can be built in various bonds. The strongest is called *English bond* and consists of one course of stretchers followed by a course of headers, alternately – *stretchers* being bricks with their long face sides laid along the line of the wall, while *headers* are bricks laid with their ends showing on the face of the wall.

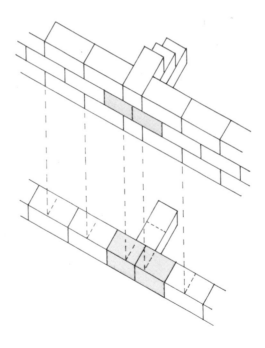

Junction of wall or buttress in half brick wall. Shaded bricks are cut to $\frac{3}{4}$ size.

Bonding of bricks requires pieces of brick to be cut. These pieces are called *closers* or *bats*. They are placed in positions where they will move the whole bricks along the wall so that they will overlap the bricks below to form the bond.

A variation of English bond which is more suitable for general building work, is *garden wall bond*. This consists of a course of headers, as for ordinary English bond, but it is followed by three courses of stretchers and then another course of headers. This bond is quite strong enough for high garden walls and sun-traps.

Cavity Walls

Habitable buildings and extensions are built with cavity walls which are two simple stretcher bond walls tied together with galvanized

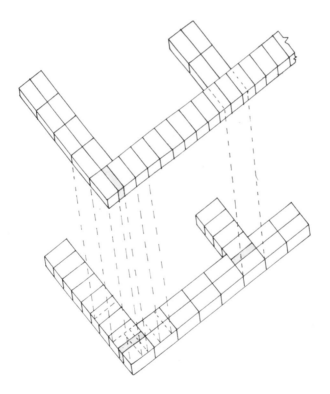

Pattern of bricks in 225mm (9 in.) wall in English bond. Shaded bricks are cut in two long ways. Dotted line shows how the alternate course fits.

metal wall ties. These ties are spaced 1m (3 ft) apart horizontally and 450mm (1 ft 6 in.) apart vertically. They should not be placed in straight rows vertically, but staggered, like the joints in the brickwork which they tie together.

The cavity of the wall should be 50mm (2 in.) wide so that the wall with its two half brick leaves and cavity will be 275mm wide, or 11 in. if imperial bricks are being used. The cavity must continue 150mm (6 in.) below the damp-proof course level and the wall ties must be kept clean and free from mortar droppings in order to ensure that the finished wall will be dry.

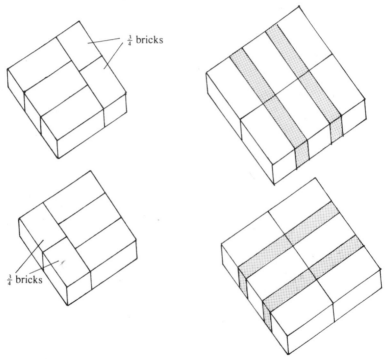

Bonding pattern for English bond piers two bricks square and 1½ bricks square, in alternate courses.

Gate Posts

Gate posts and free-standing piers must be made large enough to withstand the strain that is to be placed on them. Bonding is not their only requirement: they must have sufficient sectional area or they will break apart at the bed joints, especially at the point where the crook of the hinge is built-in. The minimum size would be not less than 330mm (13 in.) for the average gate, but a two-brick pillar 450mm (1 ft 6 in.) square is better and more able to stand up to the vibrations of the slamming gate. A coping or cap should be provided to protect the top of the brickwork and make the rain drip clear.

Any cutting of the bricks that is required can be done with the blade of the brick hammer, using a chopping action. Neat cuts for closers should, however, be made with a bricklayer's bolster, which is like a very broad cold chisel.

Apart from building walls around the boundary of the garden old bricks can be used for building low retaining walls in order to form terraces on sloping sites. They can be used for storage bins, compost enclosures and incinerators.

Other Materials

Of course, bricks are not the only materials suitable for building walls. Stone and concrete blocks can also be used if they are available more cheaply. Broken paving slabs can be obtained from the local council maintenance department and these can be squared up to form pieces about 100mm (4 in.) wide so that they can be laid like bricks. Use a cold chisel or a bolster and a lump hammer to cut them. Tap all round the slab in a straight line along one side over the edge down the other side and join up on the edge again. Twice round like this and most slabs will break. This is a knack which is soon obtained by practice.

Laying is carried out in the same way as for bricks. In some areas flints out of the garden can be used for building attractive walls. They need breaking in two so that they have one fairly flat face. The flatter types of tiles can also be used for building low walls. This uses quite a lot of mortar but if the tiles are available cheaply, they may prove cheaper than bricks or other materials.

5

CONCRETE: CASTING, FINISHES AND TEXTURES

In spite of the fact that concrete is generally considered to be hard, heavy, grey and uninteresting, it is really quite versatile and can offer a number of different surface finishes. Because it is initially a soft material, capable of being moulded, it can be classed as a plastic. Provided that the right mix is used, concrete can be moulded into most shapes, though the reinforcing of thin sections can be a problem.

Basic Materials
The basic materials for concrete are cement, sharp sand and small stones. Sand is sometimes called fine aggregate and the stones are called coarse aggregate. The cement can be obtained from builders merchants and is usually supplied in 50kg (1 cwt) bags. As the building industry has been working in metrics for some time, loose sand and coarse aggregates are supplied in cubic metres when large quantities are required. Those builders merchants which have do-it-yourself departments, and the do-it-yourself shops themselves, may sell small quantities of sand and coarse aggregate in imperial measurement. Small pre-packed quantities of cement may be obtained as well as small bags of ready-mixed dry materials for making various types of concrete and mortar. Buying loose materials from builders merchants is cheaper than pre-packed products.

Ordinary Portland cement is grey in colour, but it is possible to get white cement if the job in hand warrants the expense. Colouring materials can also be obtained in either powder or liquid form and if these are used the manufacturer's instructions must be followed exactly. This applies especially to the quantities used as the degree of colour can only be maintained by careful measurement because the concrete will vary in colour as it dries out.

Sand bought at the builders merchants will have been washed to remove dirt and impurities, so do not spoil it by dumping it in a heap on the garden. Put it on a concrete drive or path, or, if no such space is available, lay a large board on the ground to prevent the dirt getting mixed with the sand. A sheet of thick polythene will do if care is taken not to cut it with the shovel when measuring materials for the mix.

Mixing

Mixing should take place on a clean, hard surface. A platform of boards is ideal. If concrete is mixed on a path or drive, it will make a stain which will not come off. Casting should take place on a similar surface covered with a sheet of polythene to prevent the concrete sticking.

All the ingredients should be carefully measured; though almost any large tin or box can be used, a bucket is perhaps the most convenient utensil. A good general mix which is suitable for the strip foundations (not less than 150mm (6 in.) thick) of walls, and outbuildings; or for drives and garage floors, when laid at not less than 100mm (4 in.) thick over 150mm (6 in.) of well tamped hardcore, is mixed at a ratio of $1:2\frac{1}{2}:4$.

First, take $2\frac{1}{2}$ buckets of sand and spread them in a flat heap on the mixing platform. Next, take one bucket of cement and spread it evenly on the top of the sand. These two materials should then be blended together by turning them over with a shovel forming them into a new heap. This should be done two or three times until the colour of the mix is even. Then the four buckets of coarse aggregate can be introduced in the same way. All the materials are mixed dry until they are of a uniform colour.

Water can now be added. The usual method of adding water to the concrete mix is to hollow out the centre of the heap to form a crater and pour the water into it, then gradually push the ingredients into it. As the water is soaked up, the mix is turned over to ensure thorough wetting. The only problem with this is that the large quantity of water tends to wash the cement off the aggregate to form a slurry at the bottom of the crater. If the sides are breached, the cement slurry runs away off the mixing platform. It is therefore better to sprinkle water over the mix using a watering can.

Whichever method is used it is important that only enough water is used to make the mix workable enough to be put into the moulds when casting shapes, or to enable the concrete to be tamped into place in foundations or paths. Too much water will make the mix weak and will cause a degree of shrinking as the concrete dries. A mix which is too dry will tend to form air holes when it is put into moulds and this 'honeycombing' can also take place when laying foundations if the concrete is not tamped properly, though over-tamping of a very wet concrete mix can cause the cement to work to the top instead of being evenly spread throughout the mix.

Tamping

Once the concrete has been mixed it should be placed in the mould or foundation within one hour and it must be carefully tamped. Drives are tamped with a long straight edge and the resulting ribbed surface can be trowelled smooth after the initial set of the concrete has started. The surface can be left ribbed if the drive or path has a steep slope as this will provide better grip in icy conditions. Large strip foundations can be tamped with the end of a piece of 50mm by 50mm (2 in. by 2 in.) timber to compact it and remove any air holes. Obviously, small moulded objects are tamped with thinner pieces of wood and in many cases it is sufficient to use the edge of a trowel blade using a chopping action. This is useful for agitating the concrete near the sides of the mould in order to bring the cement and sand forward to form a smooth surface.

Concrete should not be allowed to dry out too quickly and the finished work needs to be covered, usually with polythene sheeting, to keep the moisture in and prevent evaporation. As soon as a cast is firm enough, the mould should be removed and if too dry the concrete can be wetted gently. Then the polythene can be replaced. At this stage any surface defects can be made good.

Making Good

The amount of making good required will depend on how well the mould has been made and how carefully the concrete has been placed in it. Concrete that has been properly tamped into moulds that have been designed so that they can be removed easily should produce casts that will need little or no making good. Although the cast may not be strong enough to be lifted, the sides of the mould can be removed after twenty-four hours. The casting may not be safe to move for three or four days or more, depending on the size of the unit. Do not be in too much of a hurry as a cracked casting cannot be repaired.

Honeycombed surfaces which have been caused by poor compaction, or by using a mix that did not contain enough fine aggregate, or which are the result of not mixing the ingredients sufficiently, should be made good with a mortar mix of the same proportions as the concrete mix, but without the coarse aggregate.

That is to say, in the case of the 1:$2\frac{1}{2}$:4 mix, the mortar is made of one part cement and $2\frac{1}{2}$ parts sand. Patching should be avoided if possible, because the patch generally dries darker than the original concrete.

Remember that cement mortar and concrete shrink slightly as they dry and harden, so use the mortar as dry as possible, because the amount of shrinkage depends largely on the quantity of water present in the mix.

Before filling the holes, all loose, thin and fragile material must be removed from the honeycombed area and if a large patch has to be filled it should be primed with neat cement grout which can be brushed into the surface. The cement mortar is immediately applied and smoothed off with a wooden float. Patches should not be smoothed with a steel float because this would darken the surface so that the patch would show even more. Don't forget that the patches will need the same curing treatment as the main concrete.

Box Moulds

Concrete blocks and paving slabs can be cast in simple box moulds made of wood. Rough timber can be used, but planed timber will not stick to the concrete so much. The most important point in making

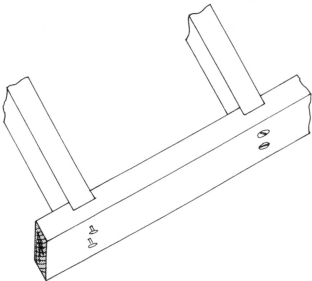

The joints of concrete moulds can be screwed or nailed. Housings hold the ends in place.

any concrete mould is to ensure that it will come apart easily after it has been filled with the wet mix, well tamped and allowed to dry.

Mould boxes can be made separately or in multiple units, depending on the amount of space available for casting. Paving slabs are not more than 50mm (2 in.) thick and can be made 38mm (1½ in.) thick for paths that will not have heavy barrows or other loads to bear. As the moulds will have to be rigid, 25mm (1 in.) thick timber will have to be used and the frame can be nailed together at the corners. Do not drive the nails right home or it will not be possible to get them out when the mould has to be taken apart. Screws can be used, but the heads get filled with dirt and cement and the slot soon becomes worn and difficult to grip with the screwdriver.

Let the sides of the mould run past the ends an inch or so as this will make it easier to tap the sides free with a hammer. The ends of the mould should be housed into the sides about 6mm (¼ in.), not so much for strength, but more as a means of keeping them in the correct position. If long threaded rods are available they are ideal for holding the mould together as they can be passed through the sides where they project beyond the ends and then the nuts can be tightened just enough to hold the box together, but not enough to make the sides bow outwards.

Do not make slabs too big or it will be very difficult moving them about to lay them. Slabs 600mm by 600mm by 50mm (2 ft by 2 ft by 2 in.) are really too heavy for the average person to move. A better size is 600mm by 450mm by 38mm (2 ft by 1 ft 6 in. by 1½ in.). Smaller sizes such as 450mm (1 ft 6 in.) square and 300mm (1 ft) square can also be made so that patterns can be laid.

Finishes
Finishes can be varied to suit whatever purpose the paving slabs have been made for. A general utility finish can be obtained by smoothing the surface of the slabs with a wooden float. This will give them a texture like fine sandpaper or coarse stone. Do not use a steel trowel to smooth the surface, because it will provide a finish which will be too slippery in winter and will soon become slimy with algae. A coarser finish for a better grip on sloping paths can be made by drawing a stiff brush over the surface when the concrete has set a little. This gives a surface of fine ridges which is not only functional, but also offers an attractive appearance when the paving is laid with the lines in alternate directions.

Where a path has to be decorative as well as functional, an exposed aggregate finish can be used. This is done by waiting for the initial set to make the concrete firm enough to hold the large aggregate in place and then taking a stiff brush and brushing all the cement and sand off the surface to expose the larger stones which are just below the surface. If the concrete is firm enough a little water will clean up the aggregate. Paving slabs finished in this manner can be dotted about the path or patio where they will look attractive, especially if they are made from coloured concrete.

Blocks

The same kind of finishes can be applied to building blocks. These can be made in wooden moulds, but it is not necessary to make them as large as the professional concrete building block which is 450mm by 230mm (18 in. x 9 in.) by 50mm (2 in.) and up to 100mm (4 in.) thick. Such blocks are heavy and very coarse to handle. Make the blocks about the same size as ordinary bricks, or a little larger, about 300mm (12 in.) by 150mm (6 in.). The thickness will depend on what the height of the wall is to be and what purpose it is to serve. Blocks 100mm (4 in.) thick will give walls comparable with those made from ordinary bricks, but 75mm (3 in.) thick blocks would still make a sound wall, be cheaper to make and lighter to handle.

The blocks can be made either lying flat on the casting area or they can be made in the upright or laying position. If a textured finish is required on one face only, then the block can be made lying flat so that the finished side is uppermost and the texturing technique can be applied. If the texture is needed on both faces, then the block will have to be made upright and the textured finish applied after the mould casing has been removed.

Finishing Blocks

An attractive finish which gives a similar appearance to natural stone can be obtained by making the blocks double width and splitting them to provide a rough surface. Cut the double block in two, after it has had time to harden, using a heavy hammer and a bricklayer's bolster chisel. A cold chisel will do if a bolster is not available. Tap all along a line right round the block, both faces and edges – in this 'green' condition it should part easily to give the required finish.

Blocks made of concrete made with large gravel aggregate will have a coarse finish however well the material is placed and compacted into the mould. A dense and even textured block can best be made using pea-shingle for the coarse aggregate in which the stones are round and smooth and not more than 9mm ($\frac{3}{8}$ in.) in diameter.

Moulds for Blocks

As the moulds for blocks will have to be used over and over again it is worth taking a little extra care in their construction. If the blocks are to be cast in the vertical position a bolt at the top and bottom at each end will be necessary to hold the sides firmly; nails will not be suitable as they will soon become too loose in their holes. Like the paving slabs, the walling blocks can be made in multiple moulds if textured faces are not required.

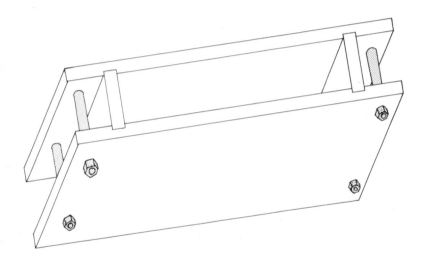

Moulds to be used many times are better bolted together.

When a lot of casting is to be undertaken and moulds are to be used repeatedly it will be necessary to oil the insides of the wood to prevent the concrete sticking to it, and special release oil can be obtained for this purpose. An alternative is to whitewash the inside of the moulds. It is also essential that the moulds are cleaned thoroughly between castings. Ordinary oil and old engine oil should not be used for release purposes, because they are likely to stain the concrete.

Fill deep mould boxes with layers of concrete about 50mm (2 in.) deep and tamp them well to compact them. Use the edge of a trowel with a chopping action at the sides of the mould to bring the sand and cement forward so that honeycombing is avoided and a smooth face to the concrete is obtained.

Copings

Apart from casting blocks and paving slabs, concrete can also be used for making the coping for the top of the walls. The copings can be either bevelled to one side or they can be made with a central ridge with a bevel to each side. The angle need not be steep in either case, 75mm (3 in.) at the centre or highest point and 50mm (2 in.) at the lowest point. Copings should overhang the wall by not less than 25mm (1 in.) at each side and a throat or drip groove must be made on the under side of the overhang as this will make the water drip clear of the wall instead of running onto it and saturating it at the top.

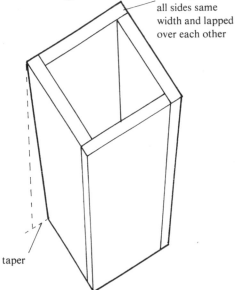

all sides same width and lapped over each other

taper

Mould for casting coping upside down, showing the loose tapered timber for producing the required slope for each side.

Copings need to have a smooth finish so they should be made with a concrete mix using pea-shingle, or they can be made from a mix of one part cement and three parts sand. It is possible to cast the coping upside down in the moulds, but although this may make it easier to form the drip groove a very great deal of care would have to be taken to ensure that the top, finished surface would be fine, smooth and without any honeycombing.

The usual way of casting copings is to place the mould boxes on a wooden base so that 6mm by 9mm ($\frac{1}{4}$ in. by $\frac{3}{8}$ in.) strips of timber (for forming the drip groove), with the top corners removed, can be tacked to the base and the mould also tacked to the base to hold it in position. The ends of the moulds should be shaped to form the top of the coping and the concrete levelled off to them.

When it has set sufficiently, that is, when the initial set has taken place, the top of the concrete can be smoothed off with a steel floating trowel. The concrete should be fairly firm so that a lot of trowelling is not needed, because over-trowelling of soft concrete will make the cement come to the surface in quantity and when dry the surface will be dusty.

As soon as the concrete is firm enough the sides of the mould should be removed and the concrete smoothed with the steel float if required. The ends will not need to be smoothed as any roughness there will help the jointing mortar to grip. Corner copings and end copings, of course, will need all their exposed faces smoothing.

Keep the castings covered and damp while the concrete cures and after two or three days the casting can be lifted off the base, or the cast turned over and the base prised off the concrete. It is doubtful if the wooden grooving strips will pull out of the cast as it is lifted, because the concrete grips very hard. No matter how well oiled these little strips are, it will be necessary to run the point of a trowel along the corner of the timber to break away any nibs of concrete that may be gripping it. Then the wooden strip will have to be prized out of the groove. If it is not damaged it can be used again, but do not use a damaged strip a second time because the concrete will wedge itself into the hollows and will wrap itself around any projections so that the strip will have to be chiselled out of the groove.

Properly tamped concrete will grip very tightly any timber used to form holes, indents or grooves in castings, so it is essential that these timbers are tapered. The sides of the grooving timbers should be planed to a slight taper towards the top and then the top corners should be rounded off a little.

Any recesses should be made with wooden blocks which are bevelled all round. An alternative is to use pieces of expanded polystyrene as this can be melted out with a blow torch when the cast is hard. Holes for bolts can be made by wrapping paper around the bolt, or a piece of rod, so that the concrete will not grip the metal. This is not quite as good as making a tapered rod which will pass right through the concrete and mould, as the paper sometimes gets caught up with the bolt when it is being tapped out and then the bolt can only be withdrawn with great difficulty.

Castings which are made upside-down, like pillar caps, corner and end copings, are turned the right way up after a few hours, as soon as they are hard enough to handle, so that the mould can be taken off and the top smoothed. The drip groove can be taken out before the cast is turned but in this case it must be done with care or the concrete will crack. When the mould is turned over the base is removed without jarring the concrete and then the sides are removed and the loose wooden slips that have been inserted to form the shape of the top of the casting. This done, the sides and top of the casting can be smoothed with a steel float.

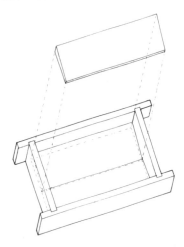

How to make a wooden box which can be removed from the concrete after it has set.

Apart from being careful to tamp the concrete well and ensuring that there will be no holes at the sides, or hollows in the middle of the casting, it is also important that the concrete is not shaken or vibrated after the setting has started, because the soft, green concrete will crack easily.

6

SMALL PROJECTS

There are those intrepid amateur builders who will tackle the design and construction of a house without having any previous experience of building, but most people prefer to start with small projects and work their way up to bigger things as their experience increases.

Bases for Sheds and Stores

Building garden walls is a fairly straightforward exercise in bricklaying and setting out bases for sheds and stores is a good simple exercise for beginners at concreting. The necessary brickwork and roof for a shed or store make a further step in the craft of building.

As with all constructional work, the first step in laying a concrete base is to clear the ground of all vegetation. The base area is then set out with string line and pegs, the first line being set up parallel with the boundary, or if necessary, at an angle to it. Another line is then set up at the exact width of the base and parallel to the first line. Next, the lines marking the ends of the base are set up. These are set squared to the side-lines and can be checked with the large wooden square illustrated in Chapter 3. A further check on the squareness of the base can be made by measuring the diagonals, which, of course, should be of equal length.

Having set out the size and position of the concrete base, the soft earth and garden loam should be dug out down to firm ground. Wooden boards should then be set up in line with the setting out strings. These boards, or shuttering, are supported by pegs driven into the ground and are fixed at the same height as the finished concrete. The top of this shuttering should be levelled so that it can be used as a guide for levelling the concrete. The boards can be about 25mm (1 in.) thick if the pegs are placed no more than about 750mm (30 in.) apart, but if thicker boards are used then less pegs will be needed. If the boards are too thin there will be the danger of them bowing outwards under the pressure of the wet concrete, however close the pegs are.

When the shuttering is in place, the area can be covered with hardcore to a depth of about 150mm (6 in.). This must be clean brick rubble, broken concrete or stones. It should be beaten or tamped down to consolidate it. When it is firm the top can be covered with a layer of clean sand. On no account should any soft material be used — no soil or vegetable matter which could rot and cause settlement.

Concreting the Area

After the hardcore has been placed and compacted, the area is ready for concreting. Bases for sheds and garages can usually be placed in one single operation. Large areas, say more than 3m (10 ft) square need to be laid in sections with an expansion joint between them to take up thermal movement which occurs during severe weather conditions. Paths, although narrow in width, need an expansion joint at about 3m (10 ft) intervals to help prevent them cracking.

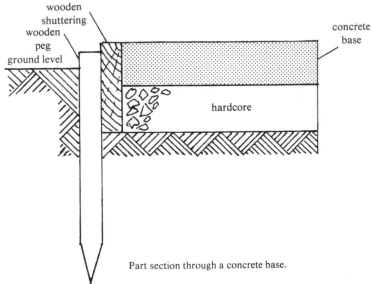

Part section through a concrete base.

Of course, there is no reason why smaller areas should not be divided up into sections to make it easier to handle and lay the concrete. In fact, if the concrete is being mixed by hand, only small sections will be possible, because a large mix would start to set before it was placed, as it would take a long time to mix and pour. Even if a small concrete mixing machine is used it will be necessary to lay the concrete in sections equal to the area which can be covered by one mix.

The depth of concrete needed for the base of a small shed can be as little as 50mm (2 in.). Workshops and larger brick buildings can have concrete bases about 75mm (3 in.) deep and garages require 100mm (4 in.) or more depending on the size of the car. The mix to use is 1 part cement: $2\frac{1}{2}$ parts sand: 4 parts coarse aggregate.

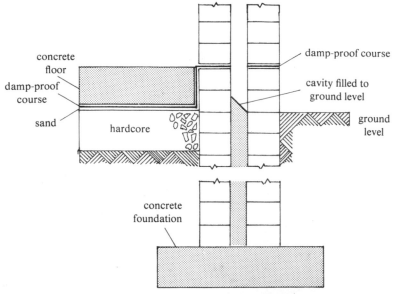

Section through a cavity wall and foundation for a habitable building.

A simple base such as the one just described is suitable for a small tool shed or a fuel store. When a more important building is to be erected, or when materials need to be stored in dry conditions, it will be necessary to insert a damp-proof membrane in the floor slab and ensure that the slab top is above ground level.

Damp-Proofing

The damp-proof membrane can be made of polythene sheeting of a thick gauge laid in one piece if possible. Joints can be made by giving the sheeting a 150mm (6 in.) overlap and either gluing the edges with a suitable adhesive or by folding the material to make a broad seam which can be held down with bricks until the concrete is placed on it. If the joint is not made properly it will be possible for capillary attraction to cause the ground moisture to creep between the damp-proof membrane and into the concrete above.

Ideally, the top of the concrete base should be 150mm (6 in.) above the ground level and, in the case of an extension to a habitable building, this is the minimum requirement of the Building Regulations. It may mean that a brick wall on a concrete strip foundation will have to be built first to 150mm (6 in.) above ground level. Then the interior of the brick box can be filled with hardcore to within the concrete thickness of the top of the wall. The hardcore should be well beaten to consolidate it. Sand can then be laid over it and the damp-proof membrane laid on top of the sand. Where the concrete is to be 150mm (6 in.) or more thick, 50mm (2 in.) to 75mm (3 in.) of the concrete can be laid and then the damp-proof membrane laid on to it before the remainder of the concrete is placed.

The damp-proof membrane should be brought up the inside of the brickwork and turned over it to form the damp-proof course for the brick wall, or another damp-proof course can be laid on top of it. As the damp-proof course of the brickwork should be 150mm (6 in.) above ground level, in the case of garden sheds with 112mm ($4\frac{1}{2}$ in.) walls it may be higher than the surface of the floor slab, and if the floor damp-proof membrane is tucked into the brickwork at surface level, this will mean that there will be one or even two courses of bricks between the floor level and the wall damp-proof course. These bricks could be subject to rising damp if the floor membrane does not completely cover the brickwork and they may present a damp face to the inside of the building. This can be overcome by bringing the floor slab damp-proof membrane up the inside of the brickwork above floor level and turning it under the damp-proof course of the wall.

The exposed polythene sheeting can be protected from damage by forming a cement and sand skirting on the inside. This can be done by tacking a temporary batten about 19mm ($\frac{3}{4}$ in.) thick to the wall about 50mm (2 in.) above the top of the polythene. Make the bottom edge of this batten as straight as possible and level or at least parallel with the floor. The batten will form a guide for applying the cement mortar and will make a straight, neat finish to the top of the skirting.

The mix to use is one part cement to three or four parts of soft sand. Apply the mortar with a wooden float and use a fairly stiff mix or the mortar will sag. It may be necessary to apply two coats to prevent sagging. In this case the first coat will have to be scratched with a nail or pointed stick to form a key for the second coat. When the initial set has started the surface can be smoothed with a steel trowel.

As the skirting will not have any key to the wall it will not withstand a lot of rough usage, but it will prevent the polythene getting torn or damaged. Take the guide batten off with care when the cement is hard.

Store Sheds and Outbuildings

Store sheds and other outbuildings are constructed in simple stretcher bond with walls 112mm (4½ in.) thick, and, of course, the brick that turns the corner presents an end to one wall face and provides the half-brick necessary to move the bricks along to form the bond pattern.

Apart from levelling the work it is important to make a gauge rod to check the height of the brickwork at the corners as they are built. The gauge rod is not measured in feet or metrics, but is marked to show the height of the brickwork at three-course intervals. Allow for three bricks, 195mm (8¼ in.), plus three mortar joints, 27mm (1⅛ in.): a total of 222mm (9⅜ in.).

If this is not done, extra mortar under the bricks at one corner can cause it to rise higher than the others and in a few courses the level would be affected and could be a whole course different. That is to say, that although the top of the brickwork could be level there could be one course more (or less) at one corner than at the others. This would make it difficult when fixing a string line to fill in the middle of the wall.

The gauge batten should be used to test the bricks at every three courses. The marks on the batten should be cut with a fine saw, so that they will not rub off. Stand the batten on the base slab if possible for measuring the brickwork, but if the slab is not level with a mortar joint, knock a nail into the lowest mortar joint at each corner and use that to stand the gauge rod on.

Door and Window Frames

Door frames are placed in position as soon as the floor slab is finished and the brickwork is built up to them. Metal angles are screwed to the door frame, level with the mortar joints, so that they can be built in to secure the frame. If the dimensions of the building can be adjusted to suit full numbers of bricks it will make construction easier as there will be less cutting. When the brickwork reaches sill height the window frames are placed in position and plumbed and levelled, like the door frames were. They are held in place with lengths of timber and they are secured by screwing metal angles to the sides and building them into the brickwork in the same way as for the door frames. A strip of damp-proof course should be placed on the brickwork under the sill of the frame to help prevent moisture in the wall rising and wetting the woodwork. A lintel is needed over the top of the window opening to take the weight off the frame. The lintel can be simply a length of angle iron on the inside of the wall for small sheds and store places where appearance is of secondary importance.

Roofs

A flat roof is probably the easiest form of roofing for the amateur to tackle as it requires no special angle cuts to be made in the timber or the brickwork.

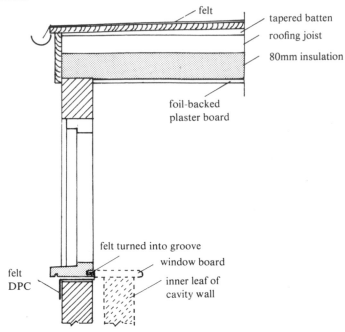

felt

tapered batten

roofing joist

80mm insulation

foil-backed
plaster board

felt turned into groove

window board

felt
DPC

inner leaf of
cavity wall

Section through a flat roof, window and single brick wall. Dotted lines
show cavity construction needed for habitable building.

Pitched roofs need the brickwork built up at the ends to form a gable and this requires skill in cutting bricks to suit the pitch of the roof. Also the rafters have to be cut at an angle at the ridge and at the eaves. This type of roof needs scaffolding as the ridge and the gable cannot be reached from planks resting on trestles.

Joists

The roof timbers of a flat roof are set at 400mm (16 in.) centres. This will meet the width of sheet materials such as plasterboard if the ceiling is to be lined on the inside. The joists should be similar in size to those of a floor, because they could be required to bear a heavy weight of snow. For instance, a floor joist 150mm by 50mm (6 in. by 2 in.) can be used to span 3m (10 ft). A flat roof of the same span would require a similar sized joist, say 150mm by 38mm (6 in. by $1\frac{1}{2}$ in.). If the depth of the joists is reduced too much the roof will be more likely to sag than if the thickness of the joists is reduced.

All the joists need to be held down by fixing galvanized metal straps to them and plugging and screwing them to the inside of the brickwork at about 600mm (2 ft) from the top of the wall. Flat roofs need to have a slight fall to get the water to run off into the gutter provided – 50mm (2 in.) in 3m (10 ft) is usually ample. This fall can be provided by nailing strips of tapered timber to the top of the joists. If about 80mm ($3\frac{1}{4}$ in.) of glass fibre thermal insulation is provided on the top of a vapour barrier, such as foil-backed plasterboard, or polythene sheets over an ordinary plasterboard ceiling (as for a habitable extension), there will be less likelihood of condensation causing problems in the roof void.

Roofing Materials

The top of the flat roof can be made of 25mm or 19mm (1 in. or $\frac{3}{4}$ in.) wooden boarding covered with roofing felt. The felt should be allowed to hang down into the gutter so that the water is not driven back by the wind to saturate the wooden fascia board to which the gutter is attached. The felt edge at the high side and the sloping edges can be turned over and nailed to the edge of the boards which should project 25mm to 38mm (1 in. to $1\frac{1}{2}$ in.) all round the roof so that the water will drip clear of the walls.

A steeper slope will be needed if the roof covering is to be corrugated sheeting of galvanized iron, asbestos or plastic. Fewer joists will also be needed because the sheeting will span wider openings. The roof would not be suitable for walking on without planks to spread the weight, either during construction or when finished. The joists need to be held down by metal straps as for flat roofs, but preventing condensation is much more difficult as the sheeting offers no insulation against differences in interior and exterior temperatures. Timber noggings need to be fixed between the rafters to give extra support if a lining of ceiling boards is to be fixed, and if a good thickness of insulation with a vapour barrier is included some success in preventing condensation could be possible.

Purlins

Supporting timbers for corrugated roofing materials run at right angles to the sheeting and are generally called purlins. The fall, or pitch, of the roof is arranged by placing each timber at a higher level in the brickwork than the previous one. The bricks between the purlins have to be cut to suit the angle of the roof so that they finish flush with the top of the timber.

The sheeting must overhang the brickwork in the same way as the wooden boarding for flat roofs. The hollows formed under the corrugations can be filled with cement and sand mortar of the same mix as the mortar used for the brickwork, or they can be filled by cutting wooden fascia boards to fit. This latter method is both time consuming and difficult. Foam plastic fillers can be bought if preferred.

The sheeting should project to about the centre of the guttering. A neat fillet of cement and sand can be applied down the sides of the roof under the sheeting to finish off the joint between the brickwork and the roofing. This will hide any badly cut bricks. Roofs like these are generally sufficient for garden sheds and stores, but of course, much more attention has to be paid to roofs for habitable extensions.

Storage Bins

The same principles of construction are used for small storage bins, except that they can be built on a slab instead of having to have a strip foundation. Fuel storage bins for instance can be built about 1m (3 ft) square with a lift-up wooden lid covered with roofing felt for the top. The timber holding the hinges needs to be plugged and screwed to the top of the brickwork and the joint between this and the lid should be covered with felt to prevent water getting through and soaking the contents. An opening about one brick wide and three courses high can be made in the front so that the contents can be shovelled out. A wooden sliding shutter is needed to cover the opening when not in use.

Brick bins can also be made for rotting out dead vegetation. The walls can either be made solid or they can be made honeycombed by spacing the bricks 57mm ($2\frac{1}{4}$ in.) apart either every course or at three or four course intervals. This open type of brickwork can be used to build an incinerator and a nearly circular plan can be adopted if preferred.

Greenhouses and Cold Frames

Base walls for greenhouses and cold frames require strip foundations similar to those of houses, but they need not be so deep. This does mean of course that they could be disrupted by exceptional weather conditions, depending on the depth that has been decided on and the severity of the weather. However, the reinstatement of these small amounts of brickwork is not a serious problem.

When building these walls it is necessary to provide some means of anchoring the wooden framework. Ragbolts built into the vertical joints of the top course of bricks are useful. An alternative is to drive an angle iron into the ground inside each corner so that the framework can be screwed to them. These irons have to be driven in after the framework has been erected, unless very accurate measurements are taken.

Cold frames are built in the same way and the sides are sloped by cutting the bricks. The glazed covers can be loosely laid on the top, or they can be hinged to a piece of wood plugged and screwed to the brickwork. An alternative to building sloping brickwork is to make the brick walls level all round and provide a wooden structure with sloping sides and hinged lights to fit on the top. This wooden frame can be plugged and screwed into place or it can be held with ragbolts in the same manner as the greenhouse framework.

It should be remembered that no buildings, small bins or store sheds built with 112mm ($4\frac{1}{2}$ in.) half brick thickness walls, can be completely dry inside all the year round, because these thin walls become saturated in winter. This means that only materials which do not need perfectly dry conditions can be stored in them. For really dry stores, cavity wall construction as used for habitable buildings is needed.

Hutches and Sheds for Animals

Timber is the traditional material for building hutches and sheds for keeping animals in, but there is no reason why brickwork should not be used, if there is plentiful supply of cheap materials. Whatever the structure is made of, it is a good idea to make the base of concrete as it is easier to keep clean and can be swilled with water and disinfectant from time to time. Such a floor should be smooth and non-slip and should slope towards a drain which has a trapped gully.

By using brickwork for the main building, the animals will be kept secure from rats and foxes. The latter have even penetrated the urban wooded parklands in some cities and towns.

Where numbers of rabbits or other small animals are to be kept in brick buildings, the walls can be sealed with a few coats of polyurethane varnish so that they are not absorbent and can be washed down when necessary. The hutches themselves would be made of timber in the traditional way. A single adult rabbit needs a hutch not less than 600mm by 450mm by 450mm (24 in. by 18 in. by 18 in.), a doe with a litter would need a larger hutch not less than 1m by 600mm by 450mm (3 ft by 2 ft by 1 ft 6 in.). Out of doors, a run with a grass floor for a single-sex litter of rabbits needs a wall 1m (3 ft) high. For nine rabbits the run would need to be at least 1.8m x 1m (6 ft x 3 ft).

The walls for these runs can be built in half brick thickness and ought to have a coping on the top to protect them from the weather. Foundations need only be shallow as any repairs needed, due to earth movement, will be easy to carry out and damage may only happen on rare occasions.

Indoor hutches should be placed on slatted shelves which will be easier to keep clean. In any case a space should be left between the back of the shelf and the wall as an aid to cleaning. The highest shelf should not be more than 1.5m (5 ft) from the floor. Rabbits do not need to have heated houses, but they should not be kept in draughty conditions.

Natural light is needed by all animals, but they should be shielded from direct sunlight. Out of doors they also need a shaded place and indoors they should be kept at a correct and even temperature. Always see that there is enough room for them – overcrowding should be avoided.

Whatever animal is being housed, there should always be doors wide enough to get a barrow through and if the animals are in pens inside the building there must be easy access to them. Where there are pens of large animals in the sheds there should be non-absorbent surfaces up to 1.5m (5 ft) up the walls. So that washing down can be carried out, do not use more water than necessary and try to keep the floor as dry as possible. Some animals will make themselves a dry bedding area if the right conditions are provided.

Windows and Doors

High windows will offer sufficient light without exposing the animals to direct sunlight. Non-draught ventilation can be provided by making a 450mm^2 (70 sq. in.) grill in the door about 450mm (18 in.) above floor level. Ridge vents should also be provided so that there will be a through current of air without causing draughts. All opening windows and ventilators should be provided with fly screens. Coved cement and sand skirtings help to make cleaning easier and prevent dirt collecting in the angles. The curve can be made easily by using a bottle as a float to smooth the cement mortar into shape.

The outside door should have a metal plate at the bottom to prevent gnawing creatures like rats from entering. The bottom of the door should also fit as close to the floor as possible for the same reason. Gates to pens should be hung so that the animals cannot wriggle under them; if the gates are hung on bands and hooks, the top hook should be fixed pointing downwards so that animals like pigs cannot get their snouts underneath any rail and lift the gate off its hinges and escape.

A good aid to hygiene is to fit a metal tray into a mat-well inside the entrance door so that a sponge mat soaked in disinfectant can be placed in it.

Other requirements are a large sink and cold water tap. Hot water is useful if it can be arranged. A large draining board would be required and at least one worktop with an easy-clean surface.

Brick walls for pens can be built directly off the concrete floor using stretcher bond in half brick thickness. Such walls are not likely to be strong enough to support heavy doors or gates and these would be better hung on posts set in the concrete floor. An alternative would be to build brick piers at least 450mm (18 in.) square and set hooks (from bands and hooks) into the mortar joints.

7

LARGE PROJECTS

Garages, large store sheds, extensions and other outbuildings follow the same construction principles: they are simply larger than the projects mentioned in the last chapter so they cost more in materials. They also take up a lot more time and energy.

These larger buildings all require the proper strip foundations which were described in Chapter 3. As garages, particularly those attached to the house, and habitable extensions have to meet various Building Regulations, the Building Control Officer will no doubt want to visit the site at intervals to ensure that the building is being erected in accordance with the plans which have been submitted for regulation approval.

A 112mm (4$\frac{1}{2}$ in.) brick wall built of facing bricks will provide a fairly dry wall, depending, of course, on the degree of exposure of the site. The weathering ability of the wall can be improved by rendering the outside with cement and sand mortar. If this finish is to be applied, no pointing will be needed to the exterior of the wall; instead, the mortar should be raked out about 6mm to 12mm ($\frac{1}{4}$ in. to $\frac{1}{2}$ in.) deep to form a key for the rendering.

Rendering
The rendering does not need a waterproofing agent mixed with it because this would make it set hard and it would tend to shrink and create hair-line cracks in the finish as it dried out. These fine cracks will let water through into the brickwork where, apart from causing damp within the building, it could freeze in winter and this could force pieces of the rendering off the wall.

A softer rendering will absorb some of the moisture but not enough to soak the wall. During dry spells this water would evaporate, thus keeping the wall dry. Water does not concentrate on absorbent surfaces, but tends to disperse evenly. On harder, smoother surfaces the water tends to run down in rivulets and these concentrations of water soon find cracks to run into and soak the wall, causing damp patches on the inside.

The sand used for renderings should be clean and sharp. Lime can be added to make the mortar more 'fatty'. An average mix that would suit most types of walls would be 1 part cement: 1 part lime: 6 parts sand. A straight cement and sand mix would give strong, fairly impervious rendering which would be subject to drying shrinkage. The cement-lime-sand mix would provide a rendering which would give satisfactory results under most general conditions.

Two coats are needed, the first being about 13mm ($\frac{1}{2}$ in.) thick and when firm the surface should be scratched to provide a key for the second coat. These scratch markings should be horizontal wavy lines evenly distributed. The first coat should be given time to dry out before the next coat is applied, so that the initial shrinkage will have taken place.

The finished coat should be about 6mm ($\frac{1}{4}$ in.) and not more than 9mm ($\frac{3}{8}$ in.) thick. It should not be finished with a steel float because of the tendency to cracking. It is better to use a wooden float if the finish is to be fairly smooth.

Roughcast and Pebble-Dash

Other finishes, such as roughcast or pebble-dash, can also be applied to the first coat. The first coat for roughcast should be mixed at 1 part cement: $\frac{1}{2}$ part lime: $4\frac{1}{2}$ parts sand. The roughcast should be mixed at 1 part cement: $\frac{1}{2}$ part lime: 3 parts sand: $1\frac{1}{2}$ parts shingle or crushed stone. The shingle or crushed stone should not be larger than 13mm ($\frac{1}{2}$ in.). The mix is made wet enough to be flicked on to the surface of the first coat by means of a trowel or a small wooden scoop. It takes a little practice to obtain a uniform texture with an even spread.

Because of the amount of water which can be held on the surface of a pebble-dashed wall, the first coat should be mixed either with a waterproof cement or a waterproofing agent should be added to the mix. In the latter case the maker's instructions should be followed exactly. The mix is 1 part cement: $4\frac{1}{2}$ parts sand. The second coat will be 1 part cement: 1 part lime: 5 parts sand. It should be applied at a thickness of about 13mm ($\frac{1}{2}$ in.).

The pebble-dashing is done with white spar or pea-shingle while the mortar is still soft. This aggregate can be thrown from a bucket by hand or a wooden scoop can be used. Lay sacking or polythene sheeting at the base of the wall before commencing pebble-dashing so that the many stones which will inevitably fall during the operation can be collected. These can then be washed in a sieve and used again later. Aggregate which adheres to the surface of the rendering should be tapped lightly with the face of a wooden float to press it into the surface and ensure a good bond.

Renderings are not easy to apply as a good deal of pressure has to be used when applying the mortar in order to get it to stick to the wall. There is then the problem of getting a level surface. This is done by first setting up horizontal bands or screeds of mortar to use as guides for the rest of the work. The distance apart for these bands depends on the length of straight edge which is available. The bands of mortar are straightened with the wooden straight edge and allowed to set. Then the space between them is filled in and the surface levelled off with the straight edge, using the screeds or bands as a guide. After a little practice, holding the straight edge at a slight angle, some of the excess mortar which is cut off can be caught on the board and transferred back to the mix.

It is obvious that the roughcast finishes are more suitable for amateurs to apply because, although they require some degree of levelling, unevenness due to lack of skill does not show so much. Rendering needs practice and in the initial stages quite a lot of material is wasted and the ground beneath the wall needs to be covered to protect it, especially if it is a path or drive, and to make it easier to clean up afterwards.

The inside of the outbuilding can be lined with plasterboard and if the walls are battened first at 400mm (16 in.) centres, using preservative treated timber, the void between the boards and the brickwork will act as a ventilating shaft to help keep the walls dry. Roof construction for simple stores has already been discussed and here again the same principles apply to habitable rooms, except that the material sizes and the insulation must meet the requirements of the Building Regulations (see Chapter 2).

Brick Tanks

Another occasion when rendering is needed is when a brick tank for storing rain water is built in the ground. Generally, rainwater tanks are metal and are situated above ground level so that the water can be drawn out easily. But there are some circumstances when a sunken tank is preferable, if only for the sake of appearance. Metal tanks sunk into the ground will soon deteriorate, because even galvanized metal cannot withstand the persistent action of the damp soil.

Small brick tanks can be built with half brick thickness walls, but large tanks need 225mm (9 in.) thick brickwork. This can be built in

English garden wall bond unless the pressure of earth to be restrained, because of the size and depth of the tank, makes the use of full English bond necessary. Such large tanks need to be designed by a professional building technician and require a mechanical digger and assistance with the brickwork and base.

Waterproofing Tanks

The average garden water storage tank need be no deeper than about 1m (3 ft 3 in.) or larger than about 1m by 600mm (3 ft 3 in. by 2 ft). The base of the tank would be concrete about 50mm (2 in.) thick. A waterproofing agent needs to be added. A waterproofing agent would also be needed in the rendering mix for the inside of the tank. Another way of providing a waterproof tank would be to build it with a concrete base (no waterproofer) and brick walls, but instead of rendering the inside, a large plastic sheet could be lowered into it and carefully spread over the base and up the walls. It would be turned over the top of the walls and held in place by a top course of bricks or concrete slabs in a similar way to lining a swimming pool.

The top of the tank could be covered with wood, or paving slabs if the tank is not too wide. Access will have to be made for extracting the water. This can be done either by bucket or by fitting a small pump. Water can be fed into the tank either by pipes leading through the top of the tank or the pipes can be fitted through the side. It is best to use water from the roofs of property because although it will inevitably contain quite a lot of dirt, it will not carry as much as the water from drives and paths. In any case, the tank will have to be cleaned at intervals.

Ornamental Tanks and Pools

Of course, water tanks and pools can be built above ground level and they can be made ornamental, even though they do serve a very functional purpose. They can be rendered on the inside or lined with plastic in the same way as the below ground level tanks. Ordinary brickwork can be used or the tanks can be built in stone.

Stone is an effective material to use for all kinds of walls, although it is a little more difficult to handle than bricks. The mortar mix should be a little stiffer than for bricks because the stone is heavier and it will squeeze out more at the joints. Care must be taken not to stain the work with the mortar. Plumbing can be difficult because of the uneven surface of the stonework. This can be overcome by building small pieces of wood into the joints so that they project the same amount. These can then be used to rest the plumb-level against so that the wall can be checked properly, but a great deal of reliance has to be placed on the judgement of the builder in keeping the work straight, level and plumb.

Broken paving slabs can be used instead of real stone. These are more even in thickness and can be cut to regular sizes. They can be laid to a line and can be bonded in a similar manner to bricks. The joints look effective if they are raked out about 6mm ($\frac{1}{4}$ in.) deep.

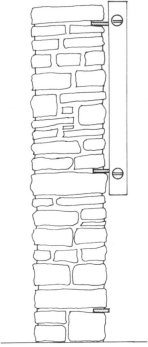

Plumbing the rough face of a stone wall using pieces of wood built into the joints.

Dry Stone Walls

If there is a plentiful supply of cheap stone (local authority depots and demolition firms are useful sources of supply), dry stone walls are interesting to build and are quite strong and durable if the work is carried out properly. It is an art that has been practised for centuries and there are many examples in various parts of the country which can be studied.

The best stones are reasonably flat and have the top or bottom square to the sides of the stone. As there is a great deal of weight in a stone wall the foundations must be strong and should be about $1\frac{1}{2}$ times the width of the wall. The concrete should be at least 150mm (6 in.) thick. Use the $1:2\frac{1}{2}:4$ mix as for brick walls. It is a good idea to fill the trench with concrete to within about 50mm (2 in.) of the ground level in order to avoid working in the bottom of a trench with heavy stones. A heavy hammer will be needed for trimming badly-shaped stones. A cold chisel would be useful for this too.

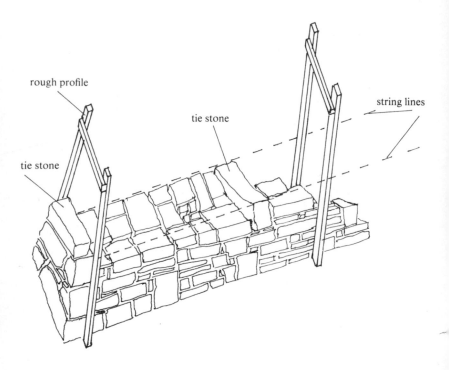

Building a dry stone wall using wooden profiles.

It is usual to slope either one or both faces of the wall to make the top narrower than the base and instead of plumbing the wall, wooden profiles are set up to the shape of the wall. These profiles, unlike those for brick walls, are made of light battens such as 50mm by 25mm (2 in. by 1 in.) and are set in the new concrete to the width of the wall base and pulled in narrow at the top to suit the slope of the finished wall.

As a guide to sizes, a wall about 550mm (22 in.) at the base and 1371mm (4 ft 6 in.) high would be about 450mm (18 in.) wide at the top. It is important to have the sides of the profiles leaning at the same angle. Making them up as a frame before setting them in the concrete helps. A plumb line should be used to ensure that they are all at the same angle. This is done by hanging the line from the centre of the top rail of the frame and then measuring at the bottom to get the same distance at either side of the line to the side of the frame.

Two string lines are then fixed to the inside of the profile frames, one at each side of the wall, and about 230mm (9 in.) or 254mm (10 in.) from the foundation concrete. The lines must be level across the width of the wall.

Building starts by laying large stones, dry, on to the foundation, using stones with a good face-edge and sighting them into place between the string lines and profiles. Once the first two courses have been laid, then lines are raised about the same amount and again levelled across.

The rough stones cannot be levelled and plumbed, but a bond should be formed as much as possible by lapping the stones over the joints of the course below. Building continues by bringing up one side of the wall and then the other, filling in the centre as work proceeds. It is essential that each stone is wedged from the inside of the wall if they tend to rock about, and very few stones will be found that do not move. A supply of small stones and rubble for this purpose, and for filling the centre of wide walls should be kept handy to make work easier.

Tie stones, which go right through the wall from the front to the back, should be placed at about 1800mm to 2m (6 ft to 7 ft) apart horizontally and about 1m (3 ft) apart vertically in the wall. They need not be placed at regular intervals and can be allowed to project a little in front of the face of the wall if necessary. As work proceeds you will get a feeling for the need for the tie stones. These stones help to strengthen the wall and they can be any shape or thickness provided that they span the wall. Other large stones called 'jumpers' can be inserted from time to time and these will add a bit of character to the wall.

When the wall reaches the full height it is topped off with a course of stones bedded in mortar. These stones should be large enough to span the width of the wall and should be as regular in size as possible. The mix to use is 1 part cement to 4 parts soft sand. A plasticizer can be added to make it easier to use. If this is done, follow the maker's instructions exactly.

If the end of the wall does not butt against another structure, it should be built square across and tie stones should be laid at about three course intervals.

The supply of stones for walling should be placed at about 600mm (2 ft) from the wall face to give sufficient room for working. A great deal more guesswork is used for curves in stone work than with brickwork. It helps if the profiles are set closer together, say about 600mm (2 ft) to 1m (3 ft) apart, but the string-lines will not be very helpful, except to keep the courses level across the wall.

If this technique is followed, the result should be a permanent and attractive as well as functional feature for the garden.

8

DRIVES AND PATHS IN CONCRETE AND BRICK

Concrete is the material usually used for laying paths and drives, which are laid very much in the same manner as the base for a garage or shed. First, the top soil or garden loam has to be cleared from the site down to firm ground. The depth is not so important for paths as they have little weight to carry, but drives need to be firmly based, because the weight of the car passing over a narrow strip at each side of the drive will cause cracking and settlement if the ground is soft.

Drives
A drive needs to be a minimum of 1800mm (6 ft) wide and the concrete needs to be a minimum of 75mm to 100mm (3 in. to 4 in.) thick. It is laid on a base of well-compacted hardcore made of broken bricks and stones. This layer of hardcore should be not less than 75mm (3 in.) thick and it is covered with a layer of sand well rolled to compact it.

Wooden boards are set up along the sides of the drive and held in place by 50mm (2 in.) square pegs driven into the ground on the outside of the boards. The boards, or formwork, should not be less than 25mm (1 in.) thick and the pegs should not be more than 760mm (30 in.) apart. The boards should be set to the necessary falls so that the water will run away quickly. Large areas of concrete need a proper arrangement of drains and gullies, but a straightforward drive with earth on at least one side can be laid with a fall to that side. With earth on both sides the drive can have a camber, that is, it can be raised 12mm ($\frac{1}{2}$ in.) to 25mm (1 in.) in the centre and given a curved surface so that the water will run off to either side.

Gullies
Where gullies are provided, and they are often necessary where drives have a fall towards the garage, they have to be positioned before any concreting starts. The gully is set in position about 25mm (1 in.) below the level of the formwork and is bedded in concrete to hold it in place. Drainpipes with a diameter of 100mm (4 in.) are laid to a fall of 1:40, their joints being packed with hemp and then filled with cement and sand mortar which is neatly bevelled off around the pipe. The drain is

taken to a soakaway which should be positioned at least 3m (10 ft) away from any buildings.

Laying the Drive

It is best to lay the drive in sections of not more than 3m (10 ft) long to minimize the risk of cracking through thermal movement. A temporary board should be set up across the path at this point and this can be removed later when the concrete has set and the next batch is ready for laying. These sections can be adjusted so that they can be laid in about one hour. If ready-mixed concrete is to be obtained, then all the joint boards, side boards and clear access for a wheel barrow and for the delivery lorry must be ready, because the driver will want to unload his truck as quickly as possible. This will leave you with a 'mountain' of concrete that must be laid quickly to avoid it starting its initial set before it is in place. The section boards in this case can be quite thin as concrete can be placed at each side at once to prevent them bowing. They will not be removed afterwards.

For drives, the concrete mix to use is $1:2\frac{1}{2}:4$ cement, sand and aggregate. It is made just wet enough to be placed and tamped without being too sloppy. Fill the drive with concrete to a height about 19mm ($\frac{3}{4}$ in.) above the level of the side formwork. The concrete is then tamped down with a length of board which will reach from one side of the drive to the other. Use the board with a chopping action. It will take two people to do the job properly and when the chopping has tamped the concrete almost level with the side forms the action should be changed. Rest the board on the side formwork and draw it up the path using a sawing action to cut the concrete off level and draw the excess forward in front of it. Where a curved, or cambered surface is required, the underside of the tamping board has to be hollowed about 25mm (1 in.).

When concreting in batches it will be necessary to fix a temporary board across the path at a point where the batch will finish. The surface of the drive can be left as it is with the rough ridges across it for extra grip if the drive has a fairly steep slope, or it can be smoothed when the initial set has started. The finishes can be the same as those for paving slabs. Trowelling with a steel float will give a surface that may be too smooth for safety in winter. A wooden float gives a rougher surface. If exposed aggregate is decided on, the surface of the drive should be swept with a soft brush about an hour after the concrete has been placed. Allow the concrete to continue to harden until the stones cannot be dislodged; it can then be brushed with a stiff brush and sprayed with water to clean the stones and leave them standing proud of the concrete surface.

Real and Imitation Slabs

Imitation paving slabs can be made by marking the surface of the concrete by rubbing the rounded edge of a piece of 6mm ($\frac{1}{4}$ in.) batten on the surface to form small grooves to the desired pattern. Crazy paving patterns can be made in the same way.

Real paving slabs can also be used for drives, but they need to be laid on a concrete base of the same type as that just described, except that the concrete need be only 75mm (3 in.) thick. The paving slabs are then laid on a bed of mortar made of one part cement, and three or four parts sand. It is possible to lay a paving slab drive over an old established gravel drive which has been well rolled, but there will always be the danger that some of the slabs will crack under the weight of the car.

Garden Paths

Garden paths are, of course, made in the same way as drives, except that they are narrower and do not need quite as much thickness of concrete. The path should not be less than 600mm (2 ft) wide and if it is a path that will be used as access for a pram it should not be less than 760mm (2 ft 6 in.) wide. Because of the expanse of concrete, drives have to be laid to proper falls, but paths do not have to carry such weights and have few drainage problems so that they can be allowed to follow the contours of the land to a large extent. It is still necessary to remove all the soft garden soil and lay a base of hardcore, which must be well rolled to form a firm foundation. Wooden boards to form the side formwork are needed and they are held with pegs driven into the ground as before.

These side forms can be set so that the finished concrete will have a fall to one side or they can be levelled across and the concrete surface can be given a slight curve or camber. This is done by hollowing out the tamping board about 12mm ($\frac{1}{2}$ in.). The concrete mix for paths can be a little less coarse than the one used for drives and can be one part cement, two parts sand and three parts coarse aggregate. A thickness of about 50mm (2 in.) is sufficient for most paths, but 75 mm (3 in.) can be used where the ground is soft or the paths will have unusually heavy weights to carry.

Concreting can be carried out as for drives, either by setting everything in place and then having the concrete delivered ready-mixed, or it can be done in small batches. Section joints will be required to reduce the possibility of cracking and these can be 1800mm to 2440mm (6 ft to 8 ft) apart. Use section boards of the same dimensions as the side formwork and then the concrete can be laid in alternate sections so that there need be no waiting for the concrete to set before carrying on with the work. When the concrete has set, the boards can be removed and the empty sections filled. Where the concrete is obtained ready mixed, the whole path will have to be laid at once, of course, so the section boards will be thin, as for the drives, and they will be left in place.

Fill the path to about 12mm ($\frac{1}{2}$ in.) about the level of the side forms and then tamp it down, finishing off with a sawing action as for the drives. The rough, rippled surface left by this method is not likely to be acceptable for paths in domestic gardens so one of the textured finishes will have to be applied.

Do not forget that with all concrete, whether it is in paths, drives or castings, the project has to be covered over as soon as the concrete is set sufficiently so that it will not be marked by the polythene sheeting. Keep it covered for two or three days and then take off the polythene and wet the surface if it has dried out.

Cobble Stones

Cobble stones can make a decorative feature and as they are uncomfortable to walk on they can be used to discourage people walking in certain places. They can be used for instance to discourage short cuts across lawns by placing a wide strip of cobbles along side the path.

The concrete base is laid first in the same way as the path. A mortar mix of one part cement and three parts sand is spread over the base and the cobble stones are set in it. The stones should be about 75mm (3 in.) or more in size and are each placed by hand in the wet mortar, bedding them to about half the depth of the stone.

Only small quantities of the mortar should be made up at a time and this will depend on the rate at which the stones are bedded. Lay the mortar topping as soon after the base concrete has set as possible as this will improve the bond between the concrete and the mortar.

Paving Slab and Brick Paths

Paving slabs and bricks make excellent paths. They do not necessarily need to be laid on concrete, they can be laid on a bed of firm sand. If heavy vehicles use the paved area the slabs, bricks or crazy paving, must be laid on a concrete base. All slabs need to be fully bedded or they will crack under the weight if a simple 'dot' method is used.

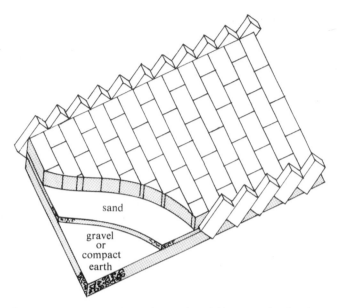

Section through a garden path in bricks laid to stretcher bond, showing edge bricks set at an angle.

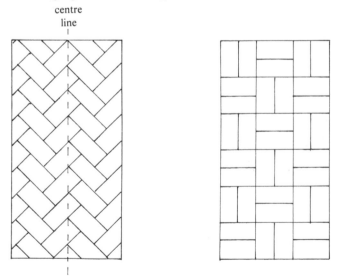

Two fancy bonds for garden paths in brick. Left, herringbone, right, basket pattern.

The base for laying the bricks or slabs in sand is started in the same way as for concrete drives and paths, by removing all the vegetation and the top soil. Hardcore of broken bricks is not needed, but coarse gravel should be laid over the area and rolled well to make it hard and firm. When the base is solid, about 25mm (1 in.) of sand can be laid over it and the paving bedded on it. This method reduces the likelihood of the slabs cracking, but getting them level can be difficult. It is easier to lay a small trowelful of sand in a heap at each corner of the slab and one in the middle. The slab is then placed on to these heaps and gently bumped down to the required level with a heavy mallet or the end of a short length of timber.

A string line down each side of the path will serve as a guide both for direction and for level. Slabs should be levelled individually and a straight edge should be used as well to check three or four slabs at a time to ensure that they are all level with each other.

Edging

In order to keep the sand under the slabs and prevent it from washing away in wet weather, it will be necessary to provide some form of edging to the path. This can consist of wooden boards treated with preservative that finish flush with the surface of the paving, or purpose-made concrete edging bedded in a weak mortar mix. This edging can be rounded on the top edge and can stand about the level of the paving. If the edging is allowed to stand proud of the surface of the path, some of the joints must be left open in order to let rainwater run off the path.

Laying Slabs

If an edging is not wanted, the paving slabs can be laid on the same compacted base but bedded in a weak mix of lime and sand mixed at one part lime to four parts sand. The sand content can be increased to six parts to make an even softer mix. Where a lot of water is expected, or a great deal of use is anticipated over the area, some cement can be added but the mix should not be stronger than 1 part cement: 3 parts lime: 12 parts sand. It can be used as dots or as a full bedding for the slabs.

Whatever method is used to lay the slabs, it is best to lay them with about 6mm to 12mm ($\frac{1}{4}$ in. to $\frac{1}{2}$ in.) joint. These joints are filled in when the area is complete. The filling can be of dry mortar of the same mix as the laying mortar, or sand can be brushed into the joints. This will bed surprisingly hard in the open joints. Filling the joints with a wet mix of mortar is not an easy task and if a cement type of mix gets on to the face of the paving slabs it could stain them permanently. Paving laid on a bed of sand, restrained at the sides, will provide a sound surface for many years. If eventually one or two of the slabs become uneven or start to rock about, it is not difficult to take them up and rebed them.

Crazy Paving

The less formal crazy paving can be laid in the same way as the full-size pavings. Pieces with straight sides should be picked out and laid along the sides of the path where they will fit neatly against the edgings. This type of paving lends itself to winding paths and irregular shaped areas. It is, of course, cheaper than the formal paving.

If crazy paving is laid in a cement: lime: sand mortar, the paths can have ragged edges filled in with plants. When the border plants spread on to the stones, they will make the new path seem an old established part of the garden.

Do not be too formal in laying crazy paving: the path will look best if the pieces appear to have been scattered haphazardly with joints of various widths. Pieces which are fitted too carefully tend to make the path look like a neat fitting jigsaw puzzle. Do not forget to give the path a little slope to either one or both sides to let the water run off otherwise pools will occur at any low parts. Crazy paving paths do not need to be quite so smooth and level as the formal paved paths, but a spirit level and straight edge should be used to keep them fairly level.

As the joints of the crazy paving are much wider than those of formal paving, it is best to fill them with a mortar mix instead of just sand. Very wide joints can be filled with a wet mix if care is taken in the application. Whenever paths are laid in mortar or have mortar filled joints they should not be walked on for a day or two until the mortar has had time to set, otherwise some of the slabs may be pressed down into the bedding and leave an uneven finish.

Brick paths are ideal for gardens as the rustic red fits so well with the surroundings. Not every type of brick is suitable for paths: the soft, common bricks soon crumble away in the wake of the winter frosts. Hard bricks can be laid flat with the broad surface uppermost and in this way they will cover more ground; but the softer bricks should be laid with their face-sides upward as these generally have a better surface for wear and for turning the water.

Any of the ways of laying paving slabs can be used for laying bricks, but because the bricks are so small a full bed of mortar or sand has to be used: it is not enough just to lay dots. The foundation for the brick paths is of course the same as for the other paths, and some form of edging is necessary in order to restrain the outer bricks.

Laying Bricks

Bricks need not be laid with open joints, they can be pushed up close to each other. These small units, like crazy paving, lend themselves to curved paths, circles and irregular areas. If a mortar joint is wanted, a thin board can be placed between each course to provide the necessary even joint. It can be taken out later and the open joint pointed with a dry or damp mortar mix.

Bricks lend themselves to pattern making and can be laid in straight courses, herringbone, or basket pattern. Herringbone pattern needs a line down the centre of the path to keep the points of the pattern in line. Basket pattern is simply two bricks laid horizontally and two beside them laid vertically if the bricks are laid with their broad flat surface upward. If they are laid on their sides there will be three needed to equal the height of the three vertical bricks.

It is not necessary to level brick paths accurately as they often look better if they are allowed to follow the contour of the land. A minimum fall for paths is 1 in 60, but a more generous fall will help the path dry out quicker and will also discourage the growth of moss and lichen which, although attractive in many ways, can become slippery and dangerous.

When bedding the bricks, they should first be set up about 6mm ($\frac{1}{4}$ in.) above the finished level of the path so that they can be tapped down level and a straight edge should be used to keep the courses in line and to keep the surface reasonably level. A popular form of edging for brick paths is to stand bricks on their ends and bed them in mortar. These bricks look even more effective if they are tilted in the direction of the path at an angle of between 45 and 30 degrees.

The bricks are cut with a hammer and bolster chisel or a cold chisel. They can be trimmed with the chisel side of a brick hammer. Some patterns, such as herringbone, need more cut bricks than others, like stretcher bond. Paths of any kind near to the house should not be allowed to cover any air vents leading to suspended wooden floors, and, of course, the finished surface of the paths should always be 150mm (6 in.) below damp-proof course level. Sand brushed over a completed brick path which has close joints will fill up the small gaps and will become very firm and compact.

9

METRICATION, MATERIALS AND MIXES

A metrication programme was started in the building industry some years ago and today most of the materials used are produced in metric sizes, and although there are builders merchants and do-it-yourself shops which are prepared to measure and sell materials in imperial sizes to meet their customers' requirements, the waste produced has to be paid for, either directly or indirectly. This is an unnecessary expense that can be avoided if metric measurement is used when planning projects.

Wastage

Much timber can be wasted, for instance, if a project requiring floor joists is planned in imperial measurement because the standard lengths of timber increase by 300mm, not by 12 inches as they did when imperial measurements were used. Timber lengths have not been rounded off to the nearest length equal to the old 1 foot increments. The shortest standard length of 1.8m equals 5 ft 10½ in., not 6 ft. Therefore, if a home extension measuring 15 ft is planned, the standard 4.5m length of timber for roof or floor joists will be only 14 ft 9½ in. and may be too short. The next metric size would be 300mm longer at 4.8m. This in imperial measurement would be 15 ft 9 in., and would result in 9 in. waste.

Standard Lengths of Softwood

The cross-sectional sizes of timber are nearer to their imperial equivalents. Timber is now 25mm thick, which is about as close as it is possible to get to 1 in., so that there is very little difference between the old 2 in. by 1 in., which was so popular with do-it-yourself enthusiasts, and the new 50mm by 25mm which is only fractionally smaller. This small amount does matter, however, when accurate and close-fitting work such as furniture making is being undertaken. When various rails, uprights and other members are added together the small differences also add up and change the overall size of the cabinet or other object.

The basic merchant's sizes of sawn softwood are from 75mm to 300mm in width and from 16mm to 300mm in thickness, with some limitations on the larger sizes. There are, of course, many other sizes

Smaller sizes cut to meet demand		Approximate width in inches								
		3	4	5	6	7	8	9	10	12
Approximate thickness in inches	Thickness in millimetres	Width in millimetres								
		75	100	125	150	175	200	225	250	300
$\frac{5}{8}$	16	X	X	X	X					
$\frac{3}{4}$	19	X	X	X	X					
$\frac{7}{8}$	22	X	X	X	X					
1	25	X	X	X	X	X	X	X	X	X
$1\frac{1}{4}$	32	X	X	X	X	X	X	X	X	X
$1\frac{3}{8}$	36	X	X	X	X					
$1\frac{1}{2}$	38	X	X	X	X	X	X	X		
$1\frac{5}{8}$	40	X	X	X	X	X	X	X		
$1\frac{3}{4}$	44	X	X	X	X	X	X	X	X	X
2	50	X	X	X	X	X	X	X	X	X
$2\frac{1}{2}$	63		X	X	X	X	X	X		
3	75		X	X	X	X	X	X	X	X
4	100		X		X		X		X	X
6	150				X		X			X
8	200						X			
10	250								X	
12	300									X

Sawn softwood cross-sectional sizes.

available, but these are cut by merchants from their stock sizes. This applies particularly to the small sizes used for general purposes.

Think and Work Metric

It is important to think and work metric because there is no easy and exact conversion from imperial to metric, and although imperial sizes are given in this book along with the metric measurements they can only be approximate and are for comparison only. For instance, 100mm is generally used as the equivalent of 4 in. and 50mm as 2 in.; but if the conversion is worked out using the conversion factor of 25.4 then 4 in. becomes 101.6mm and 2 in. becomes 50.8mm. This difference is so tiny that it does not matter until much larger sizes are converted and then the anomalies show up. Fortunately, 8 ft by 4 ft converts very closely so that board sizes which are now 2440mm by 1220mm are the same as the previous imperial sized boards.

Just as the nominal size of the imperial brick (9 in. by $4\frac{1}{2}$ in. by 3 in.) included the mortar joint, so the nominal size of the metric brick (225mm by 112.5mm by 75mm) includes the joint. The actual size of the brick itself is 215mm by 102.5mm by 65mm. This is slightly smaller than the imperial brick, but it can be used with existing brickwork by slightly increasing the size of the mortar joint.

Modular Metric Bricks

Some manufacturers are producing what are called modular metric bricks and the most common sizes of these are 200mm by 100mm by 100mm and 300mm by 100mm by 100mm. These bricks are not, of course, compatible with imperial brickwork and should be only used where new detached buildings are being erected and where metric measurements are to be adhered to throughout the whole structure and its fittings.

A similar situation exists with concrete building blocks, where two sizes (448mm by 219mm and 397mm by 194mm) are made which correspond with the imperial (18 in. by 9 in. and 16 in. by 8 in.), including mortar joints. These are available for use with existing imperial brick and block work. The sizes of metric concrete blocks are:

Nominal	Actual
400mm by 100mm	390mm by 90mm
400mm by 200mm	390mm by 190mm
450mm by 200mm	440mm by 190mm
450mm by 225mm	440mm by 215mm
450mm by 300mm	440mm by 290mm

There is a range of seven thicknesses from 60mm to 215mm (actual sizes), but not all the block sizes are made in all the thicknesses.

An important point to note is that if metric measurements are used from the planning stage, and the building is carefully designed, all the metric sizes will co-ordinate. The brick sizes tie in with timber lengths; eight bricks will measure 1800mm, which is, of course, 1.8m and the same length as the shortest standard length of timber. Add another four bricks and the length becomes 2700mm (2.7m), which is another standard timber length. This also applies to the concrete blocks. Six of the 400mm size equal 2.4m, which is a standard timber size, and the same applies to four of the 450mm blocks, which equal 1.8m. This means that by adjusting the building sizes so that the correct numbers of blocks or bricks are used, a great deal of benefit can be derived from the metric system, both in saving materials and in speeding the work, because materials planned carefully will fit together like a jigsaw.

Glass and Paint

Glass is metricated and its thickness is no longer measured by its weight. The thicknesses are now 2mm (18 oz.), 3mm (24 oz.), 4mm (32 oz.), 6mm ($\frac{1}{4}$ in. plate). Plastic guttering is also available in metric lengths of 2 metres and 4 metres. Section sizes are measured in millimetres.

Paint is another building material which is sold in metric measurement and the half or 0.5 litre tin is the nearest to the old imperial pint, one litre being about $1\frac{3}{4}$ pints. The new and equivalent old sizes are 250ml ($\frac{1}{2}$ pt.) 500ml (pt.), 1 litre (qt.), 2.5 litres ($\frac{1}{2}$ gallon), 5 litres (one gallon). Not all paints are sold in the smallest size. The approximate spreading capacities, in square metres on non-porous surfaces, are:

	Primer	Gloss	Emulsion
5 litres	60	75	90
2.5 litres	30	37	45
1 litre	12	15	18
500ml	6	$7\frac{1}{2}$	9
250ml	3	$3\frac{1}{2}$	$4\frac{1}{2}$

Loose Materials

Many loose materials are now sold in metric weights. For comparative purposes there are just over 28 grams to the ounce and 1000 grams (1 kilogramme) is about $2\frac{1}{4}$ lb. For larger quantities, 1 cwt is about the same as 50kg and the metric tonne, which is 1000kg, is slightly less than the imperial ton. Fortunately, the 1 cwt bag of cement and the present 50kg bag of cement are close enough in weight not to make it necessary to change the quantities when making up mortar and concrete mixes by weight or by volume as it is still possible to calculate one bag as $1\frac{1}{4}$ cubic feet or 0.03m³ (cubic metres).

Sand, plaster and cement are materials which are obtainable in small quantities, usually pre-packed in 5kg, 25kg and 50kg bags. But it is always cheaper to buy sand and coarse aggregate in larger quantities loose from the builders merchant. These materials will keep for just as many years as they can be kept clean and free from impurities. Cement and plaster are, of course, cheaper if they are bought in 50kg bags, but they do not keep. Damp will get to them quite soon, and though care in keeping the bags sealed will help to prolong their life, damp will eventually cause these materials to go hard.

After about six months a small trial batch mix should be made up and allowed to set, if it will. These powder materials do not need to be solid to be useless – even while they are still in powder form they can have been ruined by dampness in the atmosphere which will prevent them from setting properly.

Planning and Costing
When embarking on a project, particularly a large one, it is necessary to know what quantities of materials will be required, so that some idea of the cost can be worked out and so that materials can be ordered in good time and a shortage of materials avoided when time is available to do the work.

One tonne of cement: lime: sand mortar will be enough to lay about 850 to 1000 bricks, but this depends on the thickness of the mortar joint and on the size of the frog or indent in the brick. The same amount of mortar will lay about 600 building blocks of a nominal size 450mm by 225mm by 100mm. If imperial bricks are being used there will be 48 to the square yard. If metric bricks are being used there will be 60 to the square metre. When modular metric bricks are used there will be 50 per square metre if they are 200mm by 100mm by 100mm, and 33 per square metre if the bricks are 300mm by 100mm by 100mm.

When mixing concrete, the required amount is found by multiplying the area by the thickness to be laid. For instance, a path 9m (30 ft) long and 750mm (2 ft 6 in.) wide and 75mm (3 in.) thick would require 9 x 0.750m x 0.075m = 0.5m³ (approximately). Using a mix of 1:2:3, one bag of cement 0.035m³ (1¼ cubic feet), plus 0.07m³ (2½ cubic feet) sand and 0.1m³ (3¾ cubic feet) coarse aggregate would produce 0.15m³ (5½ cubic feet) of concrete. To get the required half a cubic metre of concrete it would be necessary to multiply this by four and buy four bags of cement and four times the amount of the other ingredients. It is always best to over order because the total volume of mixed concrete is appreciably less than the total volume of the dry ingredients, and this must of course be taken into account when the materials are ordered.

Mixes

There are two main concrete mixes. The mix for foundations, drives, garage floors and solid floors for home extensions, is 1 part cement: 2½ parts sand: 4 parts coarse aggregate. The mix used for garden paths, for casting thin objects like paving slabs and for making steps or garden pools, is 1 part cement: 2 parts sand: 3 parts coarse aggregate.

Be careful not to use too much water when making the concrete because it will weaken the finished product. Too much water can also cause the finished surface to be dusty. The mix should be just sufficiently wet to be workable enough to be placed in the formwork and compacted without leaving air pockets. Quantities are measured by volume and not weight, so it should be noted that wet sand 'bulks up'. Because of this, the sand should be consistently damp, not dry or over wet.

There are almost as many mortar mixes as there are types of building bricks and blocks. A good general mix that is suitable for use with bricks, concrete blocks, calcium silicate bricks and masonry, is 1 part cement: 1 part lime: 6 parts sand. It can be used at all times of the year. In summer the mix can have more lime and sand because weather conditions are not so severe during the early stages before the mortar has completely hardened. The mix would then be 1 part cement: 2 parts lime: 9 parts sand.

A strong mix for hard, load-bearing bricks for earth-retaining walls and work below ground level, such as water storage tanks, would be 1 part cement: 3 parts sand, with a little plasticizer added. Lime can be added instead of plasticizer and this would make the mix 1 part cement: ¼ part lime: 3 parts sand.

When making lime mortar, the sand and the lime are mixed first. Enough material for a week's work can be made up and stored. Cement should be added only to small quantities, about as much as can be used in about two hours. For a 1:1:6 mix, 1 part of cement would be added to 7 parts of the mixed sand and lime. Do not try to add water in an attempt to keep workable a mix that has started its initial set.

All mixing for concrete or mortar should be done on a clean board or on thick polythene sheeting, otherwise it will stain the concrete.

Any type of container can be used for measuring the ingredients. For large quantities a bucket is most often used, but for small quantities a one litre can would be useful because with the metric system cubic quantities can be changed easily into liquid measure, simply by moving the point three places to the right (i.e., multiplying by 1000). Using the figures for a concrete path given earlier, the cement ($0.035m^3$) becomes 35 litres, the sand ($0.07m^3$) becomes 70 litres and the coarse aggregate ($0.1m^3$) becomes 100 litres. It can be seen that these quantities would probably be best measured in buckets, but it demonstrates how easy it is to change small quantities so that an ordinary paint tin can be used as a measure. Cement is added to the lime and sand while the mixture is still dry and then thoroughly mixed before adding water.

Measure out the sand on to the mixing board and make a neat heap. On to this place a measured amount of lime and mix them by turning them over together to form a new heap. Then turn the new heap over again in the same way. Do this several times until a uniform colour has been achieved. From this heap remove enough to make mortar for about two hours work (the exact amount will depend of course on your ability as a bricklayer). The required measure of cement is then placed on top of the heap and it is turned over again in the same way until the colour is uniform once more. Water can then be added to the mix.

Make a hollow in the heap and pour water into it; work this into the dry mix adding a little more water from time to time until the required consistency is reached. Be careful not to add too much water as a sloppy mortar would be useless.

Rendering mortar is made in the same way as bricklaying mortar, but the mixes are slightly different, they vary according to the strength of the walls to which the rendering is to be applied. Where the walls are made of dense strong materials a strong rendering mix is used. This would be 1 part cement: $\frac{1}{2}$ part lime: $4\frac{1}{2}$ parts sand. The second coat can be a little softer at 1 part cement: 1 part lime and 5 parts sand. If the wall is in a sheltered place this mix can be used as the first coat and then the second coat would be 1 part cement: 1 part lime: 8 parts sand.

For general use on most types of bricks for internal or external application a mix of 1 part cement: 1 part lime: 6 parts sand is suitable. Internally, a finishing coat of gypsum plaster, neat or with sand, can be used. Externally, the finish can be roughcast or wood float finish.

When the finish is to be pebble-dash then the first coat needs a waterproofer added, following the manufacturer's instructions exactly. The mix would be 1 part cement: $4\frac{1}{2}$ parts sand, to make this mix a little easier to use $\frac{1}{2}$ part of lime can be added. The second coat can be 1:1:6.

In sheltered positions the mix can be made 1 part cement: 2 parts lime: 9 parts sand. This will generally be suitable for most types of bricks and blocks and will take a wood float finish or it can be scraped and textured. Never attempt rendering when there is any likelihood of frost, as it will be very difficult to protect the work until it is set sufficiently to withstand the temperature.

Hard cement renderings are not often used internally. They may be suitable for stores and workshops, but in habitable extensions gypsum-based plasters are generally used. British Gypsum make 'Thistle Browning' which can be mixed with three parts sand and used as the first coat on masonry and brickwork. For concrete blocks it is mixed with two parts sand. It should not be applied more than 12mm ($\frac{1}{2}$ in.) thick. The finishing coat is 'Thistle Finish' which is applied about 3mm ($\frac{1}{8}$ in.) thick using a wooden float. When the initial set starts, the surface is trowelled smooth with a steel float. In the final stages a little water splashed on the surface with a brush will wet it sufficiently to enable a fine polished surface to be achieved, but too much water and too much trowelling will result in a dusty surface. Cleanliness is important when using these materials as dirty water, dirty sand and dirty equipment will speed up the setting time and weaken the plaster.

When mixing gypsum plaster, first half fill the bucket with water then add the plaster stirring all the time. Beat the mixture well either with a stick or with a large wire whisk. It should have a consistency like thick cream so that it will just pour from the bucket. Wash the bucket thoroughly in clean water before mixing a second batch.

10

HIRING TOOLS AND EQUIPMENT

When the decision to start a project has been made and the materials for the job have been chosen, there follows the problem of providing the tools and equipment needed to carry out the work. Those persons setting out on the do-it-yourself trail for the first time will have to buy the very basic tools like hammers, screwdrivers, chisels and a saw, but the established handyman will have invested a great deal of money over the years to build up a tool kit that is equal to the range of work which he is competent to carry out.

Certainly, owning a comprehensive kit of tools for several trades can be a great convenience: a good set of plumbing equipment ready to hand is worth its weight in gold when a burst pipe pours water through the ceiling in the middle of the night. However, most of the occasions when tools, ladders and scaffold towers are needed are not emergencies, or should not be. That is when the investment value of the equipment is called into question.

Assessing Your Needs
Is it really worth keeping so much capital locked up in the garage, tool shed or workshop when there are so many other demands on your money? An investment is only worthwhile if the thing invested in appreciates in value. Tools do not. Nobody will give a good price for a well-used electric drill or a worn smoothing plane. The only other time that investment is worth while is when the object invested in produces a return greater than its depreciation. In the case of tools and equipment the return is the saving achieved by making things instead of buying them, or by using them to do work instead of employing expensive professional labour. So when assessing whether a particular tool or piece of equipment is worth buying, the important question is 'How often will it be used?'

As more and more skill in the use of tools is acquired, interest in the tools themselves will increase and there is the danger of becoming a collector rather than a user. The time to really take stock and consider the necessity of each item of equipment is when you are drawn to visit exhibitions, spend hours reading catalogues and while away the lunch hour looking in tool shop windows.

Hiring

There is no doubt that some tools will repay their cost almost the first time that they are used, but more special tools have to be used regularly to pay for themselves. For instance, there is little sense in spending a lot of money on a dowelling jig just to make one bookcase out of chipboard, or to buy a special butt gauge for door hinges just to hang one door.

This is really the essence of the question, when to hire and when to buy. Apart from the basic hand tools like screwdrivers and hammers, which are the tools that are essential to the really handy handyman, the possibility of hiring is worth considering. Providing a kit of basic tools for most of the trades which are likely to be tackled will cost a fair amount of money, as they should be the best that can be afforded – though this can be spread over a period of years.

Specialized Needs

The real money wasters are the extremely specialized tools, either hand or powered, and the heavy equipment like scaffold towers and concrete mixers. These are all very useful and possibly essential when carrying out a project, but they become liabilities afterwards, if only because of the storage space they take up. One answer may be to buy these items when they are needed and to sell them when the job is finished. But, getting back anything near what has been paid for them is impossible in most cases and the process of advertising them in the local papers will further reduce the return.

Hiring is the best way of providing these rarely used items and there are hire shops in most towns. Where there is no actual shop the local do-it-yourself shop or builders merchants is usually an agent and can get the equipment required.

Just what can be obtained, how long or short the hire period, and how much it will all cost will, of course, be subject to variation, depending on the locality and the hire firm. The major hire firms can supply just about every conceivable piece of equipment needed for every task, from laying a carpet to retiling a roof, or from laying the drains to papering the new extention.

Hiring Periods

Hiring periods vary and some items can sometimes be hired for only a few hours, but in most cases the minimum hiring time is one day. A lower rate can be expected for subsequent days and the weekly rate can be expected to be less than a series of daily hirings. It may seem that hiring for a week would allow for those delays which seem to occur inevitably, but careful organization and preparation can save quite a lot of money by keeping the tools busy and allowing them to be returned in the shortest possible time.

To get the most out of hiring, the aim should be to have the hired equipment in use for as much of the hire period as possible. This is an occasion when the handyman's time really is money. One point to remember is that a sharpening charge may be made for tools that have become dulled or damaged through use. Tools which are used to apply substances have to be thoroughly cleaned after use.

There is little point in hiring a small, domestic electric drill. Unless there is no intention of building up a tool kit for future use, this tool will have so much potential value that it would be better to buy one. If, on the other hand, a large plumbing job, such as fitting central heating, is to be undertaken, then hiring a drill of larger capacity than normal may be worth consideration.

Plan Ahead
Before hiring, it is wise to work out the positions of the large holes that will be needed so that they can all be drilled at once and the drill returned. It may be cheaper to hire it again later if some holes cannot be drilled until the job is nearly finished. Always study the price list carefully, as two or three daily hirings can be nearly as expensive as the weekly rate.

Routers and similar tools are also good subjects for hiring because of their usefulness for certain operations which are rarely carried out. There may be a charge for the cutters, which will be supplied at manufacturers prices, and this may make the tool uneconomic for very small jobs which would have to be undertaken by hand cutting.

Scaffolding and Ladders
Scaffolding, such as access towers, makes an ideal subject for hire, because it is needed only about once every four or five years when the outside of the house is decorated. Storage between uses would take up a lot of garage space and a great deal of money would be lying idle. Towers four feet square and high enough to provide a safe working platform for reaching the eaves and gutters can be hired weekly, and though the price may seem high, it has to be weighed against the high cost of the scaffold. There would probably be a lifetime of hirings in the purchase price of such an item.

Whether or not to hire ladders is a matter for personal decision.

Ladders which, like tower scaffolds, would only be used once every five years may as well be hired. Much depends on the size and age of the property that is to be maintained. A large house built in the 1930s or earlier might need regular work around the eaves and chimneys, which would make owning a ladder a sound proposition. Sectional ladders can also be useful for reaching ceiling and walls above high staircases.

It must be pointed out that tower scaffolds, indeed any kind of scaffold, must be based on firm ground. Wheels can be obtained for use where the tower can be moved over concrete drives and patios; but wide, thick planks should be placed under the tower legs when they have to stand on grass or soft ground. Ladders must be tied at the foot and at the top to prevent them sliding. This applies especially when one is working alone. When an assistant is available he or she can stand on the bottom rung of the ladder to steady it and provide the weight needed to prevent the ladder foot moving.

If a new extension is being built, then there may be a need for adjustable steel props to support the structure of the house while a steel beam is inserted into what was the external wall of the house to form an opening through to the new room. These props can be hired as well as an electric hammer to make the work of knocking down the existing wall easier.

Concrete Mixers

Concrete mixers are also pieces of equipment which, though not essential if there is plenty of muscle power available, do make the task so much easier. Again, this is an item that should not be left standing idle while preparations are made for its further use. It is essential, if money is not to be wasted, to ensure that everything is ready for the concrete and that the necessary materials are on hand.

Getting a mixer of the right size is another point to consider. To mix the concrete for a new drive a 4/3 mixer, with an output of 3 cubic feet, could be used. For paths a small mixer of, say, 3/2 capacity would be sufficient. This would have a capacity of 3 cubic feet of dry materials and produce 2 cubic feet of wet concrete. The 4/3 mixer is known as the 'half bag' because it will take sufficient fine and coarse aggregate to mix with half a bag of cement.

Safety

Safety is an important aspect with all mechanical equipment and scaffolding. Care must be taken to site long electrical leads where they will not trip people up, and leads used outdoors should have weatherproof connectors. Always unplug a power tool before making any adjustment to it because, if it becomes switched on accidentally while fingers are near cutters, serious injury can result. Even the most innocuous looking drill can prove dangerous if the whirling chuck becomes entangled in some loose or hanging material.

Power tools must never be left unattended where children are about. This applies also to such machinery as concrete mixers, for although they have no cutting edges and they turn slowly they are just as dangerous where there are unsupervised children.

Ladder safety has already been mentioned, but apart from tying the ladder at the top and bottom, there is the correct angle to be considered. A ladder should be one foot from the wall for every four feet it reaches up the wall. Also a ladder used for access to a scaffold should project above the platform level by about four feet so that there is something to grip while stepping from the ladder to the staging.

Ladders should only be used by one person at a time and they should not be used as work platforms for any great length of time: a tower scaffold gives better and safer conditions. Do not use ladders that are too short. It is not safe, for instance, to try and clean a gutter from a ladder that only reaches to just under the eaves.

Similar precautions should be taken with steps. It is not safe to stand on the top of a pair of steps, because it is easy to lose your balance when there is nothing to steady your legs against. Also it is easy to turn around unwittingly and step down over the back of the steps.

Access Equipment

The selection of the right access equipment can make an enormous difference to the time a job takes and to how well it is done. Steps should not be used for reaching heights of more than about 2.4m (8 ft) to 3m (10 ft). Trestles can be used for similar heights, but used in pairs with planks to make a platform they provide a better working scaffold. Planks supported by brackets attached to two ladders are only suitable for the lightest use. Ladders should not be used at excessive angles in order to overcome obstacles like projecting bay windows — use a tower scaffold or a purpose-made scaffold.

INDEX